Boström's *Philosophy of Religion*

CHRISTOPHER JACOB BOSTRÖM

PHILOSOPHY

OF RELIGION

TRANSLATION WITH INTRODUCTION

Victor E. Beck | Robert N. Beck

NEW HAVEN AND LONDON: YALE UNIVERSITY PRESS, 1962

 PREFACE

THE ORIGINAL RESEARCH and translations for
this volume were done by my father and submitted to
Boston University in partial fulfillment of the require-
ments for the Ph.D. degree as a dissertation, "A Translation of C. J. Boström's *Philosophy of Religion* with a
Critical Commentary" (1947). For this book, the translation has been re-edited, and an introductory essay has
been written to present Boström and his philosophy to
English readers.

The translation is the third part of Boström's lectures
on religion, the first two of which deal with theology and
anthropology. All these lectures were recorded from class
notes and edited by Sigurd Ribbing, one of Boström's
students, in the volume *Chr. Jac. Boström's föreläsningar
i religionsfilosofi* (Stockholm: P. A. Norstedt & söners
förlag, 1885). Boström's Introduction and his Philosophy
of Religion (pp. 1–18 and 192–260) comprise the body of
the translation. Boström himself wrote an *Outline of the
Philosophy of Religion* [*Skrifter af Christopher Jacob
Boström*, 3 vols. (Upsala: Victor Roos, 1883; Stockholm:
Adolf Johnsons förlag, 1901), 2, 215–36], and it is included here as an appendix. Also appended to help the
English-speaking reader are a Glossary and an annotated
Bibliography.

R. N. B.

CONTENTS

INTRODUCTORY ESSAY

1. Biography

CHRISTOPHER JACOB BOSTRÖM was and in many ways remains Scandinavia's most independent thinker. Though almost unknown in the English-speaking world, he was the only Swedish philosopher to found a school of philosophy; and, in the words of Johannes Ljunghoff,

> it is certainly no exaggeration to designate the days of the glory of Boströmism as the "classic period" in Swedish philosophy. Never has the study of philosophy stood higher in our nation than at that time. Scientists, teachers, ministers, poets, authors, and statesmen, each in his profession, and according to his ability, endeavored to make fruitful the doctrines that their revered teacher in practical philosophy once had taught them, as he kindled in their youthful souls a spark of enthusiasm that never died.[1]

Boström was not only, however, a teacher who influenced his native Sweden; in the unique elements of his idealistic vision and his incisive examinations of the particular areas of human experience—especially religion—he can make a claim to a position in the general stream of Western philosophy.

Yet for most readers the question "Who was Boström?" will be asked because of the paucity of information about him in English and of his general lack of recognition in philosophical circles. A few English reference works such as the *Encyclopaedia Britannica*, *Webster's Biographical Dictionary*, and Baldwin's *Dictionary of Philosophy and Psychology* accord him brief mention; and he is treated

---

1. Ljunghoff, *BSP*, 11–12. An explanation of the bibliographical references is given in the Bibliography below, p. 177.

at somewhat greater length in the histories of philosophy by Ueberweg, Eisler, and Höffding. His absence from Hastings' *Encyclopedia of Religion and Ethics,* however, is striking. No translations and few studies of his works have appeared in English. In 1892 L. H. Beck wrote a dissertation at Yale University on "A Comparison of the Doctrines of Reality in the Philosophies of Lotze and Boström," and John Nosco submitted a dissertation on "God in the Philosophy of Christopher Jacob Boström" to Columbia University in 1957; but these works have not been published and the amount of actual translation of Boström in them is very limited. *The Reader's Guide to Periodical Literature* discloses but one article mentioning Boström, "Sweden's Contribution to Philosophy" by Axel Lundeberg.[2] Beyond this, there is apparently no research on Boström in English. In Scandinavian countries, on the other hand, interest in Boström has been extensive. Books by or about him make a library of more than fifty volumes. He has also been translated into German.

Boström did not lay great stress on the biographies of thinkers. He believed that their thoughts, if they really had any, comprised the real element of their lives, and were all that was worth leaving to posterity. For himself, Boström lived in his thoughts. Wikner says of him that he walked the Alpine heights of speculation with perfect calm, apparently unconscious of the abysses that yawned to the right and to the left below him. There was in him a sublime naïveté and, in the best sense of the word, a childlike confidence in the omnipotence of truth.[3]

Boström wrote a brief autobiography in connection with a résumé of his philosophical system.[4] This is ap-

2. *The Open Court, 41* (1927), 410–23.
3. *STB,* 15.
4. *SB, 3,* 479–80.

parently what he wished to have known about himself, and it is herewith given in free translation.

He was born at Piteå, Sweden, January 1, 1797. At the age of nine he was adopted as a foster-son by an uncle on his mother's side, the naval architect Erik Nordlund, by whom he was supported as he attended the grammar school at Piteå. At the beginning of 1812 he went to college at Hernösand, where his interest in philosophy was aroused by the lecturer N. M. Berlin.

As a consequence of this interest in philosophy, he enrolled at Uppsala University in the summer of 1815, and remained there as much as his means permitted. The professors in whose instruction he was most interested were Biberg and Grubbe. Both while at college and at the university (until 1829), he practically supported himself by tutoring, spending in fact several years away from Uppsala for this purpose. For this reason he did not receive the Master's degree until the spring of 1824. At graduation he received the highest honors. During the next few years he studied theology at Uppsala University.

In 1827 he discontinued the study of theology and went back to philosophy, and at the beginning of 1828 he was appointed lecturer in practical philosophy. He was undoubtedly the most active lecturer in the university, and also the one most in demand. This continued until the beginning of 1833, when he was appointed tutor for the royal family and moved to Stockholm.

In the fall of 1837 he returned to the university as associate professor in philosophy, and the following spring he was appointed professor. In September 1840 he succeeded Professor Samuel Grubbe in the chair of practical philosophy, and at the beginning of 1842 he was appointed a full professor in this department. In this position he continued until the time of his retirement. During his incumbency philosophy rose to a very high position in the life of the university. In the year 1853 he was created Knight Commander of the Order of the North Star.

Dons says that Boström became fatherless in childhood,[5] which explains his adoption by an uncle. His mother lived to a ripe old age. Dons also accords Boström the tribute that it was not only in the professor's chair that he was a philosopher, but also both at home and away from home, and even on the sickbed. In everything that came into his experience he saw new occasions for continued research or for verification of results already attained.[6]

Boström suffered from physical illness during a good portion of his life. In his letters to students and associates he complains frequently of the fact that he had been prevented from doing as much as he wanted to due to sickness.[7] He died on March 22, 1866, at the age of 69. He had already been pensioned some years earlier.

Boström was apt to be intolerant with those who differed with his views. In many instances he said of them that they did not have the capacity for the study of philosophy. His argument with Borelius[8] caused Höffding to speak of his "sneering reply"[9] and to remark laconically, "You are wrong, Zeus, because you become angry."[10] Dons also, with subtle irony, says that Boström's philosophy is only for those for whom it is sufficient that the master has said it.[11] But they who knew him most intimately said that it was not from any ill will that he sometimes spoke and wrote in such words, but rather from

5. *OB*, 5.
6. *OB*, 7.
7. *SB, 3,* 489.
8. *SB, 3,* 181–245.
9. *FS, 5.* "Hånende svar."
10. Ibid. "Du har uret, Zeus, ti du bliver vred."
11. *OB,* 78. "Mesteren har sagt det."

a sense of duty to what he considered to be the truth.[12]

There could also be tenderness in his words, and there was a spirit of optimism in his soul. When his mother died, he wrote a letter to his sister that breathes genuine warmth and devotion: "Our beloved Mother has left the earthly [habitation] since I last wrote you; she has moved to a better world, where she will reap the reward of all the good she has perfected according to God's will."[13] To a niece he wrote on the occasion of her marriage:

> One ought to make as reasonable demands on life and what it has to offer as possible . . . and not expect all or even much of it. . . . By the use of this rule of life I have never found myself dissatisfied or unhappy, but have been the happiest and most fortunate person in the world, so that not even my infirmity has been a disturbing influence. . . . But it is certainly not my intention to teach you any kind of contempt of the world or indifference to the advantages in life. These, too, are the gifts of God that we should seek earnestly, receive gratefully, and enjoy wisely. One does not indeed live chiefly to have a good time, but in order to fulfill the most important duties of life. But the one can easily be united with the other, and it is a great mistake to think that our Lord begrudges us our happiness. He himself is the fountain of joy and of every other good thing, and sorrows and afflictions do not proceed from him. . . . Remain, therefore, as far as you can, a healthy and hearty individual, because thereby you please our Lord as well as your fellow men.[14]

12. So Wikner, in *SB, 3*, xxiv, note, 541–42.
13. Larsson, *MÖB*, 44.
14. Ljunghoff, *BSP*, 9–10.

This robust attitude toward life he maintained to the end of his days. In 1861 he wrote: "The only thing I regret is that I shall stop at work half done, and that I would have the mental ability to do much more, but lack the physical strength."[15] At another time he wrote: "For my own part, I am remarkably calm, because I am satisfied with what happens. For nearly ten years I have been ready to pack up; and these latter years that I have lived I have regarded as borrowed time."[16] In 1862, only a year before he retired, he wrote to a friend: "But God be praised for what has been. I am now 65 years, and can soon retire. I have the joy of seeing others continue what I have only been able to begin. Thus I have not lived in vain."[17]

For Boström his work as professor at Uppsala University was always his chief task; everything else was subordinate.[18] His duties there were heavy, but though his strength was limited he carried on his teaching with the devotion of one who loves his work. His lectures aroused great enthusiasm in his listeners. Edfeldt speaks of his genuine personality and the earnestness and love that characterized his public and private teaching, as well as his entire life. Of Boström it was true that "Nemo potest inflammare alios, nisi ardet ipse."[19]

Nyblaeus has described Boström as a teacher in these words:

> At the beginning of his lecture, after he had adjusted his glasses, he produced a long and narrow pamphlet from which he now and then sought guidance for his line of thought. His voice was usually somewhat

15. *SB, 3,* 521.
16. "Haft på köpet." Larsson, *MÖB,* 53.
17. *SB, 3,* 523.
18. Leander, *LGI,* 2.
19. *SB, 3,* xiv.

weak and faint as the lecture began, but gained in strength and firmness as he continued, without, however, overstepping the boundary of harmonious proportion. At times he would raise to his chin the gold-headed cane that he used for his promenades. After the lecture was concluded he would step down from the chair with a slight bow to his listeners, and with the same courteous and kindly smile as the one with which he had taken his place.[20]

Closely related to his work as a teacher was his writing. Boström was often distressed about the fact that the demands of his duties as a teacher, together with physical weakness, prevented him from writing. Sahlin expresses regret that he made the request that papers left at his death, for the publication of which he had not made definite provision, should be destroyed.[21]

In his writing Boström insisted on brevity. He said, "If the metal that has been acquired is genuine, it does not need much volume to be of value."[22] It was generally believed when Boström died that he had left extremely little writing. But as his editors began to collect his various papers it was soon discovered that the output was not as meager as had at first been supposed. His works comprise three large volumes and afford a quite complete presentation of his philosophical system.[23]

Boström's style is plain and transparent. There is a classical simplicity in his writings, as there was in his extemporary delivery, that cannot but affect the reader and convince him of the earnestness of the thinker.[24] Wikner,

20. *FFS, 4,* Part 1, 6.
21. *SS, 10* (1917), 10.
22. *SB, 3,* 552.
23. Nyblaeus, *TUBF,* 2.
24. Beck, *RLB,* 13.

evaluating Boström's style, makes the observation that he cannot be compared with Plato in the playfulness of fancy, the flexibility of his thoughts, and his fine irony. But he adds that when Boström could devote himself to his thoughts in peace, and give expression to them from his own point of view, he could be likened to a son of Hellas in artistically clear and measured plastic.[25] Although Boström did not himself write his *Philosophy of Religion*—it was edited from class lectures by Sigurd Ribbing, one of his students, and it is therefore not always so clear and concise as works from his own pen—the reader may nevertheless sense in it something of Boström's quaint and archaic, yet clear and forceful, style.

Nils Linder, in an article that gives special attention to Boström's use of the Swedish language, says that it is by its logical clarity and incisiveness, the stability of its composition, its correctness, conciseness, and unostentatious simplicity, that his style merits the attribute of artistic. He also observes that the Swedish writers are few in whom the words and what they are to signify harmonize so well as in Boström.[26]

2. *Boström's Philosophy*

Boström's high regard for philosophy is evident in all his writings. This follows from his belief that philosophy in its essence is God's thoughts, which man strives to think after him.[1] The problem of all philosophizing is to secure harmony with one's reason,[2] and so with God himself. Man's interest in philosophy, Boström holds, is a necessary consequence of his eternal essence and appears when he has reached a certain level of development.

25. *STB*, 27–28.
26. *Festskrift*, 380–81.
 1. *SB*, 2, 481–82.
 2. *SS, 6* (1913), xxxix, 12.

It is, in fact, nothing else than his interest in himself as a rational being and hence in his true life. The first and last question of philosophy is how we are to grasp or understand the absolute being, or God, and the relationship between the absolute and the relative.[3]

Philosophy is regarded by Boström as the highest and the essential science. As such, it deals with the principles of the other sciences and of their ground. This ground, as the object of philosophy, is taken by Boström to be the absolutely existing being; and indeed he believed that, in the development of his idealistic system, he was the first philosopher to have investigated the concept of being in its pure generality. The link between his conception of philosophy and his idealism is shown by Boström when he writes that "philosophy, therefore, requires a subject, and if it should reveal itself as infinite, then God alone could be its subject, and thus philosophy becomes God himself, seen, namely, as simply knowing."[4] True philosophy for Boström can have nothing other than rational beings or persons as its subjects; and, since truth is the identity of knowing and being, it can have only beings or persons as its content. Philosophy is the wisdom of God—indeed, it is God himself and his eternal ideas.

Boström holds that absolute idealism is the true and necessary world view, and that idealism in turn requires a perfectly perceiving being, or God. He writes that "originally, there is nothing else than the infinite reason and its contents, i.e., nothing but God and his eternal determinations—his ideas, or conceptions, all of which are absolutely living or self-conscious, and consequently perfectly perceiving or rational beings."[5] With most idealists, Boström does not seek the real in the realm of

3. *SB*, 2, 193.
4. See below, p. 7.
5. *SB*, 2, 270.

ordinary experience but rather in the unchangeable eternal ideas in the absolute reality. Reality is fundamentally spiritual; it consists of God and his eternal ideas, and, with St. Paul, Boström believes that it is in God that we live, and move, and have our being.[6]

For Boström, infinite reason and God are two expressions for one and the same being. Man is not reason itself, but only a rational being whose reason, nevertheless, is eternal, unchangeable, and holy. Therefore it is not reason but only the sensuous-rational man that can be depraved or imperfect when he does not use his reason.

As to his form, God has the general attribute of infinity, which is more closely determined as absoluteness, independence, perfection, system, unity, and omnipresence. In his content, considered ontologically, God has the attributes of absolute non-sensuousness, which means that he is spiritual or immaterial and eternal or nonchangeable; absolute system, which includes power, unity in plurality of being *(unitas multiplex);* and omnipotence. Considered noologically, God has the attributes of absolute reason, including absolute self-consciousness, and absolute personality, including knowledge and omniscience.

In relation to man's theoretical capacity, God is apprehended as the true; in relation to man's practical capacity, as the good; and in relation to his esthetic capacity, as the beautiful.

In his doctrine of God, it should be pointed out, Boström shows considerable kinship with the Eleatics. He says that they finally understood that motion in itself is impossible and hence cannot belong to the real. When they had to face the argument of experience, which questions neither multiplicity nor origination, they (and es-

6. Acts 17:28. Cf. *SB*, 2, 124, 341, 400, and passim.

pecially Zeno) criticized experience, and proved that, as absolute, it is more unreasonable than the Eleatic doctrine of all as one. They were able to do this because of the general validity of the Eleatic concept of being.[7]

Boström holds that that which is to come into existence must *be;* hence, that ideas originate or are *formed* by the absolute spirit only means that they are *thought* by him.[8] He further says that God is not in himself active, but rather active only in relation to man, which he considers consistent with God's immutability.[9] Thus Boström's faithful disciple, Nyblaeus, is led to observe that "the Being which in all respects is alive or absolute cannot need any development or change. It is also generally admitted that it is not the motion itself, but the independence in the motion, that reveals life."[10] It is apparent that Boström is aligned with the eternalists. There is no motion, no change, and no development in God. Because of his omniscience, he knows about development and change, but only as it appears in and through man.

In God's thoughts, the perception and the perceived, or knowing and being, are identical; in Berkeley's famous phrase, their *esse* is *percipi.*[11] The perceptions or ideas, in so far as they are thought by God, are absolute, perfect, and determinate. They are his own self-consciousness in its individual determinations. In themselves, the ideas are self-conscious, perceiving, or rational beings. They are not created by God, inasmuch as they are part of his very being; but he is regarded as their ultimate ground in whom they are all contained.

7. Ribbing, *FR,* 83.
8. *SB, 1,* 156.
9. Ribbing, *FR,* 61–62, 64–66, 78.
10. *Festskrift,* 9. See also Åberg, *BV,* 56.
11. This is a fundamental principle for Boström. On Boström's historical relations, see below, pp. xxx–xxxix.

These ideas or rational beings comprise a system, or an absolutely ideal organism. The moments that comprise a system must in relationship to the whole be more or less imperfect. In the case of self-conscious beings they perceive more or less perfectly. They therefore stand in relation to each other as higher and lower in the sense that the lower being has fewer other beings (those still lower) as its positive determinations and more other beings (all the higher ones) as its negative determinations. It is itself taken up as a positive determination in all the higher beings, whereby it has a fuller determination than it has in itself alone. For example, much more can be said about the number 10 when it is considered in the number 100 or some higher number, than when it is considered alone. In this series, the highest number would be God, who has only positive determinations.

In his ontology, it should be noted, Boström has used categories derived from consciousness. He holds that life is self-consciousness, and self-consciousness is life. Life, furthermore, is not connected with any substratum or anything substantial, but rather itself comprises the primary and substantial element in everything. This approach places Boström among the personalistic idealists. Edfeldt says of him that he started from the principle of personality,[12] and a number of commentators refer to Boström's personalism. Nyblaeus, another of Boström's students, says that his view could properly be called the philosophy of personality in a more correct and comprehensive sense than of any view previously presented.[13] Leander writes that Boström's system establishes itself as a rational idealistic philosophy whose principle is found in the idea of self-consciousness, and that seeks the true and fundamental reality in the eternal and person-

12. *SB, 1,* 49.
13. *Festskrift,* 2.

al.[14] Ljunghoff, in fact, makes the claim that Boström's idealistic personalism helped to save Sweden from atheism and pessimism.[15] And Karl Pira, a more recent sympathetic and able interpreter of Boström, observes that Boström felt that the truth that life and self-consciousness are identical was an original discovery with him.[16]

Boström's personalistic view is established by his psychological and epistemological approach to the problem of reality. His methodology is a rationalistic one in which, as he says, everything empirical and realistic has been eliminated. "In reality," he writes, "the whole method [of philosophy] consists in this: through analysis and abstraction a person goes back to the most simple element in his consciousness, and then, by means of this, he synthesizes the more concrete, in order by synthesis to illuminate the concrete with the clarity he has gained in the more abstract."[17] Sahlin observes that Boström's philosophical method is the constitutionally determined[18] form of the systematic activity of thought.[19] This constitutionally determined form reveals itself in continuous reflection, which by abstraction or analysis always leads to a development of more complete ideas in a definite sequence. This sequence has its ground in the systematic form of the original content of human consciousness, and the systematic form is the constant determinateness that leads to the activity of reason. Therefore the method of philosophical research is the systematic self-development by which a thinking person develops his original content to the highest possible clarity, and arrives at a

14. *LGI*, 4.
15. *BSP*, 13.
16. *SS, 1* (1908), vii, 177.
17. See below, p. 15.
18. "Lagbeständ."
19. *Festskrift*, 360–78. See also Wedberg, *LSBF*, 21–24; Dons, *OB*, 26–27; Ljunghoff, *BSP*, 120; Vannérus, *BTF*, 115–16; and Åberg, *BV*, 76–80.

relatively systematic knowledge of that content. L. H. Beck summarizes Boström's method thus:

> Boström aims to be speculative and philosophical in all his writings. He disregards all individual and concrete facts and dwells exclusively with his reasoning among the generals. With a kind of intellectual "Anschauung" he intuits his whole system, and then proceeds to explain its inner connection and development with great dialectical skill and astuteness. What is thus logically explained and proved is beyond question the ultimate truth.[20]

Boström's philosophy is thus both idealistic and rationalistic. His view excludes not only space, extension, and matter from the true and original being, but also time, motion, and change. Holding that nothing exists originally except God and his ideas, that nothing exists outside of God, and yet that God is the ground of finite being, Boström is necessarily led to what he considered the second part of the basic question of philosophy, the relation of the absolute and relative.

Everything impersonal, according to Boström, is only a form or manner in which the personal appears to finite consciousness. For finite man there is, therefore, beside the absolute and supersensible world, also a relative and sensuous world that belongs to him immediately and to God (through him) mediately. This latter world, in itself the faulty[21] one, is nevertheless—relatively to man—the necessary and correct *phenomenon* of the former. Since this world is the relative antithesis of the absolutely true one, its parts must be more or less temporal and transitory, existing in space (extended, external, remote), not spiritual but material, not absolutely alive but relatively

20. *RLB*, 12–13.
21. "Oriktiga."

lifeless, unconscious not free (i.e. passive), impenetrable,[22] etc.[23]

The sensuous and temporal world, therefore, finds its explanation in Boström's thought not in a creative act of God, but rather in an eternal idea in God, namely man, by whom the world is created through finite and imperfect perception.[24] Boström accepts (and frequently modifies) idealistic arguments directed toward establishing the phenomenal character of the natural order.[25] The true substance of this order is spiritual reality, screened from man, however, by his imperfect perception. "I should perceive God himself in a grain of sand," Boström says, "if I perceived it perfectly."[26] A comment on this belief are his words to the effect that in a somewhat modified form he accepts the phrase of Anaxagoras, ἐν παντί πάντα,[27] in the sense, namely, that in each individual being the whole universe is present in a certain way, just as also was the case with the monads of Leibniz.[28]

Though phenomenal, the world is not, Boström insists, merely illusion. He says that he accepts the existence of the phenomenal world as a material world, and that we have preceptions that are called sensations and are perceived[29] material things.[30] He says further that the sensuous world is certainly not a false one, provided it is not taken to be anything other than what it is—which is the case when it is taken to be the only true reality,

22. "Ogenomskådliga."
23. *SB, 3,* 14–15.
24. *SB, 1,* 245.
25. See further below on Boström's historical relations, pp. xxx–xxxix.
26. Quoted in Wedberg, *LSBF,* 154.
27. Fragment 11. See John Burnet, *Early Greek Philosophy,* 4th ed. (London: A. and C. Black, Ltd., 1930), 259.
28. *SB, 1,* 241.
29. "Senterade."
30. *SB, 3,* 234.

i.e. as anything other than man's world and manner of perceiving.[31] He also takes an unnamed writer sternly to task for having said that he (Boström) does not believe that the world surrounding us in space and time exists.[32]

Boström draws a number of implications from his view of nature. He excludes detailed study of the phenomenal world from philosophy, which for him deals only with true being. He believes that there is an infinite number of phenomenal worlds, and he often says that if there were only one world, then Hegel would be right.[33] Since what is substantial in nature is rational and nonsensuous, there are no ideas in God for plants and animals; they are only phenomena for man of rational beings. Otherwise, says Boström, man could not use them for his purpose.[34] Finally, Boström holds that to demand that this should be a better world would be to demand that man should not be man, which would be a contradiction. God therefore, Boström also concludes, is not responsible for evil, since he did not create man.[35]

In his philosophy of man, Boström rigorously pursues his idealistic tenets. Man is not a union of body and soul because he is essentially one spirit, and his body is nothing else than his sensuous and phenomenal form. Self-consciousness is the primary and substantial element in him as in all things, and as substantial, man is an idea in

31. Boström was an unyielding foe of realism. See *SB*, *2*, 270–81; *3*, 232, note 128; and Ribbing, *FR*, 20–30.

32. *SB*, *3*, 244, note 142.

33. Wikner, *STB*, 17.

34. Boström faced the consequences of this doctrine and accepted them. He says, "My idea can enter the phenomenal world of other beings and for them be impenetrable; if I become the ingredient of iron, I may be forged; if I become the ingredient of wood, I may be used in carpentry; if I become the ingredient of food, one can eat and digest me. But this does not concern me, because it does not enter my consciousness, but only into theirs." Quoted in Wedberg, *LSBF*, 180.

35. On moral evil, see further below, pp. xxvii–xxxviii and 67–81.

God. Man is rational in so far as the content of self-consciousness is God, and sensuous to the extent that the content of his self-consciousness is the phenomenal, which is the result of his imperfect perceptions. Man may have degrees of development, including feeling, consciousness, and self-consciousness. In his theoretical activity man seeks a higher self-consciousness by changing the inner man; and by the practical activity he seeks a higher independence by changing the external conditions of life.

Boström speaks of a lower and higher cognitive faculty. The lower faculty expresses itself progressively as feeling, imagination, and understanding. The higher faculty, or the consciousness of the supersensible world, expresses itself progressively as spiritual feeling, fantasy or allegorizing imagination, and reason.[36] The entire cognitive faculty is opposed to man's sensuous capacity, which expresses itself as instinct, desire, and will.

Boström sees man as a force of such nature as to work according to its own essence, viz., an idea in God, and as having the capacity of approaching relative unity with its idea.[37] Man's present life has only phenomenal reality and poses for him the task of developing and realizing his essence, rationality. At a certain stage in his development, man becomes conscious of himself as a *person*, i.e. he knows himself as an independent and conscious being. As a self-existing and self-determining being, however, man must decide in time what he is to be, the ground for which cannot be sought in anything but himself. Man's existential struggle, properly understood, is an effort toward rationality and religion.[38] Rational activity

36. *SB, 3,* 15–16.
37. So, Boström says, man does not know God because he is rational, but he is rational because God's essence is present in him.
38. Which are in fact identical for Boström. See further below, p. xli.

can have no other purpose than the realization of reason, i.e. making the absolute, rational, and divine life actual in human life, and the realization and development of the human life in the divine. The reality of reason in man is his religion, which may be properly designated as love to God and God's love to man. For man's religion is not only his love to God, in whom he beholds the purpose and goal of his activity, but also God's love to man who, through God, becomes a partaker in true perfection and blessedness, which consist in likeness to God and unity with him.[39]

Boström was a strong defender of the doctrine of human freedom, which is a corollary of his view of man as a self-determining and personal being. He speaks of freedom as a necessary condition for the possibility of morality,[40] and man's development toward his idea is better or worse, depending on the use he makes of his freedom.[41] This view of freedom is summarized by Boström himself in his own outline of his philosophical system as follows:

> Boström vindicates man's *freedom* in the usual sense of an ability to choose between antithetical grounds of determination. He [Boström] can do this with more success and thoroughness than all others, since according to his view the sensuous world is man's own possession, and since his present life is a continuing development (actualizing) of it [his idea], and is potential in his essence, or at least a consequence of it. Therefore he ought to a certain

39. *SB, 1,* 345–47; *2,* 486. Boström seems to indicate that this goal is never perfectly attained, however *(SB, 2,* 294–95), and this in turn is linked to his doctrines of immortality and transmigration.

40. *LSBF,* 246.

41. *SB, 2,* 495.

degree himself to be able to direct and determine the nature of his development after he has developed to the degree of personal power[42] or self-consciousness or independence which we designate with the words intelligence and will.[43]

Boström thus ascribes to freedom the meaning that it is not determined in advance how the decision of the will is to be made.[44]

A second view of freedom, however, is also found in Boström when he speaks of God's freedom. This latter is God's independence; and the more free man becomes, the more like God does he thereby become.[45] Hence Boström both defends man's freedom in time—defined as his ability to abstract from desires and exercise self-determination—while he is developing toward the realization of his idea, and holds to a certain determination for man in the fact that he is destined to move toward that realization. Thus, in morality man's freedom is his freedom of choice, and in religion, as he becomes like God, it is his independence.

Boström's view of moral evil is linked with his conceptions of freedom and man as person. Physical evil, it has been noted above, is present in the sensuous world; but, since the latter results from man's imperfect perceptions and not from a divine creative act, God is not responsible for such evil. Boström characterizes physical evil as the unpleasant for man that does not have its ground in man's free will but is rather a disturbance of his lower nature. Such evil, therefore, is the result of man's limitation in time as a rational-sensuous being.

42. "Självmakt."
43. SB, 2, 494.
44. Cf. Wedberg, LSBF, 248.
45. Ribbing, FR, 160.

Moral evil, on the other hand, has its roots in the will and its freedom. Hence moral evil is found only in personal beings who have the capacity of self-determining choice.[46] To be good for Boström is to be rational; evil is sensuousness and irrationality. Yet evil is a self-conscious and free activity (Boström rejects theories of evil as privation) and is a potentiality within man in his nature as a free agent. But it is not essential to man, and hence with the higher development of man evil will be increasingly removed and annihilated. In other words, evil does not possess an eternal substance and will not continue forever, since the thought of the eternal existence of evil does not harmonize with the thought of God as the absolute end of all life.[47]

Boström also holds that the consciousness of immortality in man is grounded in his consciousness of personality and his tendency to perfection. Since man's struggle is intent upon a goal that has not yet been attained (and is never fully attained because of remnants of sensuousness that remain with him), the necessity arises of a continuation of life in order to reach it. Indeed, several forms of development are necessary, for man does not feel completely satisfied in any moment of his existence—although from God's point of view, man's idea is perfect. Therefore it follows that a higher life than the present belongs to his existence, and man must conclude from this necessity that other forms of life are included in God's idea of him.

Thus Boström holds not only a theory of immortality but of transmigration as well. In his true being, man never begins or ends, but goes through endless forms,

---

46. More technically, Boström links evil with man as *ego*, defined as that which is identical in sensuousness and reason.

47. For the religious implications of these doctrines, see below, p. xliii.

each one of which, in itself, however, is finite. In his own summary, Boström writes:

> But he [Boström] does not regard the end of the present life as an immediate entering into the eternal, but he shows the necessity for man of still other forms of life before he can attain his highest completion in his development. Concerning these forms of life he teaches that they are from eternity potential in man, just as the present one before it became reality, and that the individual phenomenal worlds, which man has for himself under each one are not found in the space beyond, or in the time after the present, since this is in both instances empirically infinite, so that it cannot have any other outside or beside itself.[48]

Death, therefore, is for Boström only phenomenal—an expression of man's finiteness and a consequence of his temporality. In relation to a succeeding life, it is but a transition.

Boström's ethics is Kantian and Platonic. In his own summary of his philosophical system he devoted only one paragraph to ethics. The worth of the individual must be held in high regard. Man is to make his higher nature or idea the principle of his life. Moral activity is a free self-development for the attainment of life in God. In this activity, however, man's sensuousness receives a positive meaning as a means for reaching the self-development that is man's prerogative, because the activity is a purposeful, conscious, free, and rational activity that has to do directly with the control of the sensuous in man.

48. *SB*, 2, 496. See below, p. 92–94. Cf. also *SB*, 3, 290–91; and Åberg, *BV*, 57, 61, and 121. For relations to Kant's argument on immortality, see below, p. 91, 95–96.

Boström calls his ethics a *positive rational* ethical system.[49]

Boström holds that the state is a rational personal being as well as man. He defends the monarchical system and the classes of society as they existed in Sweden in his day. He also holds that his theory of the state is the most liberal of any that up to that time had been proposed, because it requires the most complete independence not only for the state itself, but for all persons in it.[50] Boström maintained a great interest in social thought throughout his life.

3. Historical Relations

Boström's writings reveal the fact that he had a thorough knowledge of the history of philosophy. His *Outline of the History of Philosophy*[1] covers the field of philosophical thought, beginning with Oriental philosophy and continuing to his own time. Hans Edfeldt, one of his intimate students who edited his works, wrote an introductory chapter that bears the significant title, "The Relation of Boström's Philosophy to the Historically Given Philosophical Systems, Which Are its Antecedents."[2] The systems included as having had influence on Boström are those of Plato, Leibniz, Kant, Fichte, Schelling, and Hegel. Although Aristotle is treated somewhat extensively by Boström in his *Outline*,[3] he is not included in Edfeldt's essay.

From Plato Boström received his system of ideas or rational idealism and the principle that being is spiritual and has the content of consciousness. He also accepted

49. *SB*, 2, 497; cf. Åberg, *BV*, 84, 88; and Sahlin, *KSB*, 100.
50. *SB*, 2, 501–08.
1. *SB*, 2, 7–144.
2. *SB*, 1, 1–92a.
3. *SB*, 2, 29–40

the Platonic doctrine that there is a non-sensuous, timeless, and eternal ground of becoming that is the ultimate
source of all development,[4] and that God is Providence
or the personal guide of man and his world. In Boström
there is also found Plato's belief that man's purpose is
to come to a clear consciousness of the ideas and their
unity, as well as of the idea of the Good, and to order
his life so that he attains the idea.

But Boström holds that Plato falters when he ascribes
moments to God that are sensuous, thus introducing a
dualism into his system of ideas.[5] He finds this to be due
to the fact that Plato's idealism is relative, since the idea
with him is not originally a subject, or person, but only
something that can be the content of a person.[6] Thus the
soul cannot be explained from the idea, because it is not
identical with it as is true for Boström.

Boström persistently maintains the distinction between the empirical and the rational. Plato thinks of the
ideas as being only the original and true content of consciousness, but Boström views them as also being themselves self-conscious and rational beings.[7] With Plato the

4. Yet this doctrine, of course, strongly reminds one of Aristotle's
unmoved mover.

5. Boström says that we must not transfer moments to the divine
self-consciousness that belong to the empirical self-consciousness, or
moments that are laws and forms of the sensuous world. *SB, 1,* 15.

6. By relative Boström means a philosophical viewpoint that begins,
not principally with the subject as such, but only with its content or
determinations. See Edfeldt, *Festskrift,* 223. Relative determinations are
determinations for the senses, and thus temporary and changeable ones.
Absolute determinations are determinations directly for consciousness,
and therefore something in themselves, necessary, and unchangeable.
SB, 1, 7.

7. Walter Pater says that in their first stage Plato's ideas are abstract,
but that in the second stage they become animated, living persons, almost corporeal, as if with hands and eyes. *Plato and Platonism* (New
York: The Macmillan Company, 1903), 152. Boström's answer would be
that there is no "as if" about them. They *are* living persons.

ideas are regarded as forms of divine reason, as spiritual objects, while Boström thinks of them as spiritual subjects.

Pontus Wikner, one of Boström's favorite pupils who for a while was professor in Kristiania (now Oslo), draws this comparison between Plato and Boström:

> The one as well as the other has erected, not simply a city in which to dwell, but a temple in which to worship. If there is something that can be called speculative devotion, it is the feeling that grips us as we enter this sanctuary of the eternal beings. The trouble and din of the world is there silenced. Everything has stopped: the struggle and striving of life, the activity, yes, time itself. The world is reduced to a shadow, nothing more. Both Plato and Boström know that this shadow is but the obscure image of the temple; the only difference is that Boström knows *why* the shadow must fall here, that it is an optical phenomenon bounded by law. And the temple itself is very much alike in both of them. It is built of ideas, and has its completion in the idea of the good. But Boström knows that within these radiant walls there dwells a varied personal life. This life is a beholding. Every idea is a spiritual eye, and all behold each other, and are beheld by each other. But they do nothing else, and nothing happens in this temple. It is a service without ritual, without song, without words, without mobile thoughts. It is an existence without activity, a life without history. At this point the two philosophers meet anew. Twenty-two hundred years of history intervene, but they are united in banishing history from the world of truth. The question is whether man will be satisfied with the shadowy existence that is thus assigned

to him; but he will, nevertheless, admit that the prospect of a world of clarity and harmony, which Plato and Boström have opened for him, is something beautiful to think about, when he is to determine the goal, in the direction of which he is to guide the development of humanity and of the world.[8]

The philosophy of Leibniz, on which Boström did his first philosophical writing,[9] is a second important influence. Both philosophers stress the importance of personal categories; and they are in close relationship in their explanations of the physical world by imperfect perception. Also, Leibniz views the monads as centers of force, and Boström ascribes the same quality to the ideas.

Leibniz and Boström differ, however, in their conceptions of God's relationship to the outer world. For Leibniz God is the source of the best possible world; Boström holds that the ideas are eternal in God, who stands in a mediate relationship to the world, in and through man's spirit, for which the sensuous world is immediate. Boström says that the system of Leibniz brings God into the sensuous world, whereas his own does not. When Leibniz conceives of God as thinking of all possible worlds, then they could also be in God's consciousness, there possessing harmony as an ideal reality. God could then have created them all, provided his will is not weaker than his understanding—although for Boström the idea of creation is impossible, and is not explained by Leibniz. Boström holds that an infinite number of worlds is not only

8. *STB*, 28–29. See also *SB, 1*, 5–25, 109, 311; Leander, *LGI*, 120–23; Beck, *RLB*, 10; and Ribbing, *FR*, 29.

9. *SB, 1*, 93–111. For further material on Leibniz, see *SB, 1*, 27–54, *2*, 77–86; Ribbing, *FR*, 29, 34–38, 54, 77, 92–96; Edfeldt, *Festskrift*, 223, 252–53; Nyblaeus, *TUBF*, 3–4; and Wikner, *STB*, 27.

possible, but is actual in God, for each one of his ideas is the whole from a certain perspective, so that he *has* within himself the perfect world. That God should choose the best possible world would not be reasonable because, if he could have them all in his consciousness he could also produce them. Thereby both the world and God would have been more complete just as he was more perfect in his thought by thinking them all. Boström believes that the correct part of Leibniz's view is the teaching that the world that is God's is absolutely perfect, and that the imperfect worlds are already contained in it as to their possibility. Thus comprehended, the position of Leibniz becomes like Boström's.

Boström further criticizes Leibniz's philosophy as relative, by which he means that it is not concerned with the subject alone, but with its content and determinations, and that it grasps the relationship of the monads under the analogy of what is in space, or as a "spiritual mechanism." Finally, Boström finds that Leibniz's theory of pre-established harmony makes his monadology deterministic, while for him the eternal ideas in God are free and independent beings.

Kant's view of the sensuous world as phenomenal, and his doctrine of the ideality of space and time, are a part of the system of Boström.[10] Both thinkers emphasize the forms of understanding, Boström accepting the *a priori* principles of Kant, as well as his emphasis on consciousness as self-active intelligence.[11] Boström also agrees with Kant that man cannot transcend his own consciousness.

10. *SB, 1*, 54–61; Edfeldt, *Festskrift*, 224, 245–46; Nyblaeus, *Festskrift*, 2–6, 11–12; Sahlin, *KSB*, 17–18; and Ribbing, *FR*, 98–100.

11. Kant says, "Only in so far as I can grasp the manifold of the representations in one consciousness, do I call them one and all mine." *Critique of Pure Reason*, tr. Norman Kemp Smith (London: Macmillan and Co., Ltd., 1933), 154. Boström holds that it is by an independent act of our thinking that we understand anything. Kalling, *OK*, 78.

For Kant, however, the world is a phenomenon of an unknown thing-in-itself, whereas for Boström it is a phenomenon of idea as spiritual and concrete reality. Boström criticizes Kant's thing-in-itself as something lying outside of consciousness, thus creating a dualism. For Boström consciousness is reality, and therefore there can be no metaphysical dualism between consciousness and anything external to it. Kant is concerned with the phenomenal, and God becomes a postulate; with Boström, however, God is central, and the phenomenal world is the system of God's thoughts imperfectly perceived by man. Thus Boström is nearer to Berkeley and Hegel than to Kant at this point.

Boström believes that Kant performed a great service to practical philosophy in directing attention to duty; and with Kant he holds that man is to be regarded as an end in himself, not as a means only. Boström is also considerably indebted to Kant in his discussions of freedom and immortality. Especially on the latter, Boström acknowledges a correspondence between his argument and Kant's.[12] Kant holds, he writes, that man feels the unconditional necessity of continuation in moral and blessed perfection. This necessity postulates that man's noumenal being is higher than the phenomenal and, since perfection is not attained in time, infinity or immortality is required to advance toward it. Boström says he follows the same reasoning, except that his argument is taken from man's disposition in general, and not merely one—that toward morality. Furthermore, Boström holds that if man's essence should cease, the demand of reason that sensuousness should in some instances be negated would be sheer absurdity, for this demand implies that man should sacrifice his whole existence as man. Finally, Bos-

12. See below, p. 91.

tröm says that the religious belief in immortality finds verification in his view of God, wherein man's essence is an idea that, though conditioned, is so only by God. While, therefore, freedom and immortality are postulates with Kant, they may be seen as fundamental for Boström.

Boström considers the important element in Fichte to be the thought that there are no objects and no existence that can be considered as falling outside of consciousness. Self-consciousness is an independent existence without any underlying substratum, but it is rather its own substratum. Self-consciousness plus will, i.e. subject or person, is the substance, and all substance is self-consciousness and will. Boström emphasizes the identity of life and self-consciousness as the first and simplest substance in the universe, and holds that everything that exists is a form of life or self-consciousness. Beyond this, Boström has nothing essential in common with Fichte.[13]

Schelling had a great influence on Boström. In this connection mention must be made about the effect on Boström of his teachers, Biberg and Grubbe, who were themselves greatly influenced by Schelling. They held that the sensuous world had its final ground and purpose in an independent and perfect immaterial reality, i.e. in a divine intelligence. Biberg held that the ground of man must be an idea in God, and Grubbe separated God from space and time, teaching that God must be a self-conscious being, a personality. Boström was therefore directed toward giving attention to the world of eternal ideas that is found in God's consciousness, thus moving further in the development of his philosophy of personalism.

The fundamental thought of Schelling's philosophy,

13. *SB, 1,* 61–66; Ribbing, *FR,* 31, 99; Nyblaeus, *Festskrift,* 3; Edfeldt, *Festskrift,* 224, 256–57; *SB, 2,* 117–30.

which prevailed in Sweden at that time, was, briefly, that nature and man exist, not only through God, but in God. They comprise forms in and through which the Divine Being, which is just consciousness itself, thought of as an infinite activity beholding and determining itself, expresses and perceives itself. In this view, however, God is brought into time, and is subjected to its imperfections; and man becomes a dependent expression of the divine power, is bound by time, and is subject to corruption.

Boström differs and, as he holds, advances from this position by his development of the principle of idealism to the principle of personality. By this principle the self-consciousness that corresponds to its idea is not only a person, but the absolute personality itself, whose moments are composed of original or independent personal beings. But the influence of Schelling on Boström came largely through his teachers, Biberg and Grubbe.[14]

Toward Hegel Boström takes a critical attitude; but the fact seems to be that he was influenced by Hegel to a considerable degree. Boström is said to have received three principles from Hegel which are central to his system. The first is: to be is the same as to be for someone, or to be perceived.[15] The second is: nothing can be a determination without being something in consciousness. The third is: God could not be omniscient, if he did not possess the form of system. There does not, however, appear to be clarity or agreement among Boström's students in regard to the inference that Boström derived these principles from Hegel.

There is similarity between Hegel and Boström in their emphasis on reason as the highest approach to God,

---

14. *SB, 1,* 67–80, 2, 131–44; Edfeldt, *Festskrift,* 224–25, 256–57; Nyblaeus, *TUBF,* 4–17; Ribbing, *FR,* 100–03; and Beck, *RLB,* 9.

15. It is apparent that these are the words of Berkeley. See below, pp. xxxviii–xxxix.

and there are repeated statements in Boström that strongly remind one of Hegel's dictum that the true is the whole. Boström, however, frequently charges Hegel with pantheism.[16] This, says Boström, is due to Hegel's system of nature as process in one world, where man appears, works, thinks, and perishes. He says that Hegel brings God into time. With Boström reality does not include nature, which is only phenomenal—the sensuous world is the product of man's imperfect perceptions. Nor does God need a concretion in and through nature, for he is complete in himself, independent of the senses, and timeless.[17]

In their respective treatments of religion, however, there are a number of striking similarities, even though the question of the influence of Hegel on Boström is difficult to assess. Both philosophers hold that the consciousness of God is immediate in man's consciousness.[18] On the relationship of philosophy and religion, both hold that philosophy unfolds itself when it unfolds religion,[19] although Hegel's view seems to place philosophy prior to religion while Boström says that philosophy is a development in the form of knowledge of the highest religion.[20] Both thinkers also seek to relate their philosophies to Christianity.

Berkeley is one philosopher who should be added to Edfeldt's catalog of men whose thought influenced Boström. Boström was familiar with Berkeley and directs his readers to Berkeley's works. One of his central

16. For Boström's reaction to this charge against himself, see below, pp. xlvi–xlviii.

17. *SB, 1,* 79–90, 2, 321; Nyblaeus, *Festskrift,* 13–15; Wedberg, *LSBF,* 176–77; Edfeldt, *Festskrift,* 257–58; Dons, *OB,* 14; Åberg, *BV,* 44–45, 84; and Ribbing, *FR,* 61, 71, 103, 114, 117.

18. See below, pp. 13–14. *LPR,* 42–43.

19. See below, pp. 53, 56. *LPR,* 19–20.

20. See below, p. 56.

thoughts—to be is to be perceived—is, of course, the same as Berkeley's *esse* is *percipi*. He also expresses appreciation for Berkeley's refutation of the view that perceptions are images of things. Boström's major criticism of Berkeley, however, is that he could only rise to a lower empirical idealism, or to a subjective idealism, which could not reveal anything existing in and for itself in an absolute sense as the content of our perceptions.[21]

Boström's relations to other thinkers, it is apparent, are extensive and, because of his rather full knowledge of the history of philosophy, usually explicit. In this matter, he continues a tradition that has marked many of the great idealists, especially since Hegel, of intensive study of the history of philosophy and of developing a philosophical position by continued reference to other systems. Students of Boström will find his many historical allusions interesting and frequently insightful.

4. Philosophy of Religion

Boström's thought is always pursued from a religious perspective. He says that all philosophy that does not satisfy man's religious and moral consciousness must be false—a conviction that became his at the age of twenty.[1] Boström also believed that he was the first philosopher to present a truly philosophical science of religion.[2] He does not, to be sure, deny that there had been philosophy of religion in Western intellectual history, but rather his claim is that he brought this discipline to a position that it had never attained before. Edfeldt, in his survey of the

21. *SB, 1*, 279; *2*, 91, 95, 118; *3*, 218–19, note 100; Borelius, *KBF, 2*, 11, 80–81; Nyblaeus, *Festskrift,* 5; Nyblaeus, *TUBF,* 14; Wedberg, *LSBF,* 92; Ribbing, *FR,* 24–26; and Edfeldt, *Festskrift,* 223, 244, 254.

1. Wedberg, *LSBF,* 9.
2. See below, pp. 20, 24.

relation of Boström's philosophy to the historic systems, says that "any philosophical science of religion, as comprising an independent principal part of practical philosophy had not yet arisen. Boström is the founder of the philosophical science of religion."[3] The validity of this claim will, of course, be accepted or rejected in connection with his central system of philosophy.

The philosophy of religion is defined by Boström as "an attempt to determine religion by reason." It is for him, therefore, a normative discipline, and belongs to practical philosophy. Boström divides philosophy—a division in which he takes some pride—into theoretical and practical: theoretical philosophy dealing with the true or the given, and especially with the absolute as ground, and practical philosophy with the good or with what should become actual. The former includes theology, anthropology, and ethnology. Practical philosophy is the doctrine of reason as purpose and law, whose unity is religion, and it is divided into the science of religion in a restricted sense, ethics, and politics.

Religion for Boström is the central practical activity of man. It is "the consciousness of man's connection with God and his dependence on him in all the various forms of consciousness." Religion is thus basically feeling—it is man's absolute value and interest; but Boström holds that all man's rational powers, theoretical, practical, and esthetic, are radically religious. He therefore rejects definitions of religion centering solely on feeling, morality, or power, and holds that religion is man himself as a unity in all his multiplicity—a unity of feeling, willing, and knowing.

Man's reason, for Boström, is in fact his consciousness of God, separated from God, however, because of its less

3. *SB, 1,* 92. See Boström's Introduction below for his own historical survey on this point.

inclusive clarity. This separation from God and from his idea poses for man his central task, and it is religion that gives man the power to move toward the goals of holiness and righteousness, i.e. to God himself. Religion may also be seen as an activity seeking to determine the lower by the higher, the sensuous by the rational, the finite by the infinite. Such determination, again, is an activity directing man's powers to their true freedom and realization. For man, it has been noted above, is not reason itself, but only a rational being who shares God's rationality, who has knowledge (science) through participation in God's omniscience, and who has life through God's life.[4] Thus in effect Boström proposes a radical identification of reason and religion. Indeed, the very reality of reason in man is his religion, and this in turn is his blessedness and his life in God. The correct concept of religion is identical with reason itself: reason does not exist without religion, and no being is rational unless it is also religious.[5]

But religion also arouses respect for the being on whom man depends, viz. God, and Boström makes a further identification of reason and religion (considered in their purity) with God. It is, of course, God who leads man to rationality and gives his reason form, content, and life. In a variety of ways he is also the ground of all finite beings. With regard to their origin and duration, God is their original being. As ground of their development, God is their religion, their highest law and end. Thought of as a person in this relationship of ground, God is their highest regent, their providence, and their savior. The system of finite-rational beings is the kingdom of God.[6]

4. *SB, 1, 33.*
5. *SB, 1, 307.*
6. *SB, 2, 483.*

Man's religious activity, considered in its unity, centers on the worship of God[7] and leads man to the highest and most harmonious development of his functions for his highest end. Devotion is man's entire being completely filled by God. Piety is the state of mind wherein one freely subordinates one's activities to the religious demands on them. In so far as man approaches unity with God's idea of him, he approaches perfection. When, furthermore, man discovers that all his powers are in or from God, he strives to make them moments in the service of religion.

As it appears in time, however, religion often takes on what for Boström are false and incomplete forms. Such forms arise because of an imperfect relationship between reason and sensuousness.[8] Thus, atheism is theoretical or practical empiricism in religion. Indifferentism is found in the life that is not influenced by God. Formalism is placing essential importance on a certain dogma or on an external mode of action. The pietist has religion in his heart, but this piety is apt to prod his vanity in the thought of being God's pet. Mysticism is in danger of stopping at the beginning of the religious life, viz. the standpoint of feeling and immediate intuition. The danger in quietism is that the duties of life are neglected. Superstition arises when the religious activity in man is tainted with the sensuous, as in thinking of God anthropomorphically. It is also found in the popular concept of prayer and in belief in miracles, in special revelation, in predestination as an arbitrary act of God,

7. The reader will note that in his discussion of worship, Boström has the worship of the Church of Sweden primarily in mind. He observes that "a philosopher cannot readily get away from the religion into which he was born." It may be further added that Boström was a patriotic Swede (cf. Landström, *OTB*, 18).

8. Many of these imperfect forms were active in Sweden during Boström's lifetime. See Chap. IV below.

and in man's being led to a fall by an evil spirit (all of which Boström rejects). The imagination about guardian angels is a sensualizing of man's own higher nature.

True religion, on the other hand, consists in realizing one's essential nature, rationality and union with God. Judgments about truth and error in religion must be made by philosophy which, as the highest science, has the task of purifying religion. This does not mean that Boström replaces religion with philosophy, for he finds that religion is not exhausted in philosophy because it reaches the whole man and determines all his activities. As the highest science and the critic of religion, philosophy judges and winnows, though, as Boström writes, "the philosophical science of religion can just as little make positive religion superfluous as philosophical jurisprudence can make positive justice superfluous."[9]

These tenets of Boström's philosophy of religion serve as the general basis from which he moves to a treatment of the more special issues of religion. Thus Boström does not admit any fall of man or doctrine of original sin, explaining evil rather as the misuse of freedom by man because of his immersion in sensuousness. The results of evil may follow a person into his succeeding lives,[10] yet evil will be increasingly removed and annihilated. Therefore Boström concludes that the eventual salvation of all persons will be realized. He denies the doctrine of hell, seeking to demonstrate the irrationality of this belief on the basis that man is an eternal idea in God, and that he cannot fail to attain his idea. In a rather emotional article on the entire doctrine Boström concludes: "To hell, therefore, with the entire old barbaric devil-and-hell doctrine; and thither also—we were about to say, with all the crude and thoughtless beings that yet in our day pro-

9. *SB*, 2, 496.
10. Boström, it will be recalled, believes in transmigration.

claim it."[11] Evil has no eternal substance in Boström's view, nor can God in any way be thought of as the source of evil.[12]

Eventually realized by all persons, salvation is to be *won* by all. That is, man has the power to convert himself, either in this present life or in some other form of life. Boström holds—counter to the teaching of the Lutheran Church[13]—that salvation is not conceivable without man's free cooperation. The essential (and only real) sacrifice for man is to bring sensuousness into harmony with reason, a sacrifice nevertheless abetted by God because he is present in man and is active in conversion.

Revelation is given extensive treatment by Boström.[14] Faith in a special inner enlightenment and in special revelation are for him superstitions. He argues that a doctrine cannot be accepted simply because it lays claim to being revelation, and that the problem of revelation is to find some kind of validation for it. Such Boström proposes in his doctrine that revelation—be it the Christian claim or any other—must be identical with the content of reason, provided the revelation is true and divine. The rational is identical with the true; that which is not true and good is consequently not rational; the truly rational is the absolutely true; the absolutely true is the really rational—such of Boström's propositions emphasize his insistence on rationality as the core of revelation. Divine revelation is the act through which God becomes

11. *SB, 3*, 282.

12. *SB, 3*, 261–65; Åberg, *BV*, 68–73, 119–122.

13. Cf. Luther's explanation of the Third Article of the Creed: "I believe that I cannot by my own reason or strength believe in Jesus Christ my Lord or come to him; but the Holy Spirit has called me through the Gospel, enlightened me with his gifts, and sanctified and preserved me in the true faith. . ." Boström's rejection of the central Lutheran belief in justification by faith explains his lack of acceptance as a philosopher for Lutheranism.

14. *SB, 3*, 3–81.

known.[15] God originally reveals himself in a perfect way: for God's essence is present in man, making him rational. But, from man's side, this revelation must be realized successively, which realization is in turn history, seen from the highest point of view.

Other specifically religious doctrines discussed by Boström can be given brief statement, for they are mainly denials. It has been noted above that he denies the doctrine of creation: man is just as eternal as God, and what proceeds from man (nature and evil) is not caused directly by God. Boström rejects belief in miracles, in intercessionary prayer, and the authority of sacred writings. And he denies theories of election, prevenient grace, and vicarious atonement. In sum, Boström holds tenaciously to his doctrines that religion in itself is God, that God is divine reason, and that, therefore, human religion is a sharing in the divine rationality.

5. Comments

Boström's philosophical position, as well as his views of religion, are certain to raise critical reflections in his readers today as they did among his contemporaries. No full survey of these and other possible criticisms of Boström can be attempted here; yet brief discussion of some of them may be of value for introductory purposes.

Idealism, be it of Boström's personalistic variety or in other historic forms, faces two central problems: first, in establishing itself and especially in giving a satisfactory account of nature; and second, in developing a theory of the individual or—in religious terms—of avoiding pantheism. Boström, it is apparent, argues for his idealism in a relatively a prioristic manner, beginning with prem-

15. Hence all philosophical knowledge is revelation—a point which Boström develops. See below, p. 137.

ises that seem certain (at least to him) and moving from them to various idealistic conclusions. Few thinkers today will accept this methodology. Nor are they likely to accept the reduction of nature to phenomenal reality. As noted above, Boström emphasizes his belief in a material, even if phenomenal, world; yet his closest students had difficulty with his doctrines at this point. In a general way, one may say that Boström's philosophy is closer to (and perhaps more if not fully adequate to) the realm of spirit than the realm of nature.

Further comment on Boström's idealism must be foregone: the entire history of philosophy over the last hundred years is a critical commentary—sometimes destructive, but perhaps less so than some enthusiasts of philosophical fashions claim—on the merits of idealism. The second question raised above, however, is more a problem of internal criticism, and is concerned with important issues within Boström's system.

Boström claims rather boldly to have removed all dualism from his philosophy. Yet he has before him, on the one hand, the problem of the individual striving to reach his goal which is unity with his idea in God, and on the other, he is anxious to avoid pantheism. Put another way, Boström insists that the individual, finite personality is free and self-determining, and also argues that there is but one substance, viz. God. Boström criticizes Aristotle for accepting the idea of a substance other than God which, he says, is an unproved supposition. A quotation from Egon Zöller poses this problem of individuality versus union in a particularly forceful way:

> Is not filiation with God[1] the goal that we continually approach, without ever attaining it? . . . In

1. "Gottes-Kindschaft."

salvation we have attained the highest goal, namely, filiation with God. We are independent, self-conscious members in the absolute personality of God. Since we in ourselvs are independent in the eternal salvation, therefore we cannot be as God apprehends us, namely, perfect moments in the system in which God perceives himself and all that is his in an absolutely true manner. Then we would merge with God, and our individuality would be destroyed. Since we are independent, as moments in God, we must also in our eternal salvation remain distinct from God and from one another.[2]

That Boström was much concerned with pantheism is evident from the fact that some of his early writings deal with the subject.[3] In a rather lengthy discussion he attempts to distinguish his position from pantheism. He says that we have learned from our *Catechism* that God is everywhere present, which means that he is in *our* spirit. Even to speak about God, we must have him in our self-consciousness. Our religion also teaches us not only that we live, and move, and have our being in God, but also that he, who himself is a spirit, has given us of his spirit, and that he dwells in us, i.e. in our spirit.[4] Boström says that if one wishes to call this pantheism, it may be done, but that the Christian religion is then also pantheism, which he says no one is willing to admit. According to Boström's view, the sensuous world cannot exist without God, but God does not need the sensuous world any more than the real sun needs the visible sun. The spiritual is the true and original existence, and when God is

2. *Festskrift,* 112, 115.
3. *SB, I,* 157–82.
4. Acts 17:28; I Corinthians 3:16.

considered as the absolute spirit, all true existence must be thought of as in him, and he must not be placed in immediate relationship to anything external. Boström views the sensuous world as the phenomenon of the spiritual and super-sensuous world, and as standing in the same relationship to it as dusk to daylight, or the visible sun to the real sun. Boström holds that, if this must be called pantheism, it is at least not the usual kind. He takes his position to be absolutely idealistic or spiritual, and that it therefore is completely inconsistent with pantheism in the ordinary sense. So, for instance, the number 10 is independent, even though it is a determination in 20, 30, or any other number.[5] Eisler, it may be noted, calls Boström a panentheist rather than a pantheist.[6]

But it is apparent that Boström has difficulty in freeing himself from the charge of pantheism, and that the exact relation of the individual person and God is unclear in his system. Wedberg is led to remark that it is impossible from what Boström himself says to ascertain whether he believes that man finally reaches identity and union with his idea or not.[7] It thus appears that Boström only partially succeeded in clarifying the relations of the finite and the infinite.

A third question for comment concerns Boström's relation to Christianity. He claims that Christianity is the highest and final religion, and observes that there was need of a new and higher deposit in experience and life before an essentially higher step could be taken in man's philosophical development, and this deposit was Christianity.[8] Boström also claims that his philosophy is a vindication of Christianity, that it conforms precisely to

5. *SB, 1,* 399–400; *3,* 13, note; *2,* 273–74.
6. *Philosophen-Lexikon,* 72.
7. *LSBF,* 259.
8. *SB, 1,* 26.

Christianity when the latter is purified of the forms of fantasy that are found in it as a result of theology.[9]

Boström interprets the Christian viewpoint, as different from the Jewish, and freed from the empirical additions of theology, in this manner:

> God is eternal and unchangeable. He is not only God, but also man, as the Son, who is begotten of eternity. Consequently he exists, not as a production in time, which is only a symbolical expression, but as an eternal relationship. We think of the one who *has* the idea as prior[10] and the idea as latter, though both are the same in essence, and the idea, furthermore, has his own personal existence. This Son has in the fulness of time assumed human nature, or entered the sensuous world, which consequently is an immediate creation by him. It is thereby said[11] that God indeed is the creator of this world, but not immediately, but through the Son.
>
> This is, therefore, *our* view: [There are] God and his thoughts, which, as his ideas, are each himself in a determinate way (just as with me and each one of my ideas); therefore λόγος is originally ἐν ἀρχή with God, and is God, or God is he. But each such idea creates, i.e. comprehends himself as a mode[12] of life. When he thinks himself, he also perceives the entire system of God's ideas, but since he is not the absolute reason, he perceives them with determinations relatively opposite to those which they have in themselves or for God. Such an antithesis is that of succession, and the fact that *within* man's world there

9. Ribbing, *FR*, 67–68.
10. "*Prius.*"
11. "Vilket ock anmärkes."
12. "*Modus.*"

is origin, change, and corruption, and that it is completed in time. This means that in a certain period
of time each human being becomes conscious of his
world; if one gathers the whole series of his finite existence into *one*, then he must in certain moments of
it be more self-conscious, i.e. these [moments] must
for him be more present, and other [moments] less.[13]

Christianity like reason, Boström holds, is older than the
Bible. What theologians say man has received through
revelation has rather been found only in and through his
reason.[14] That is, Christian truth is accessible to man's
reason if he earnestly seeks it there and does not simply
wish to gather it from other sources.[15] Christ's own
Christianity was his deep and clear consciousness of, and
relation to, God.

But while claiming to vindicate Christianity, Boström
at the same time rejects many of its central doctrines. He
denies the Trinity and therewith the unique position of
Christ. Jesus for him is only one of God's many sons.[16]
This in turn leads Boström to deny such further doc-
trines as *satisfactio vicaria* and a special revelation in
Christ, and to interpret the redemptive element in
Christ not, as Ljunghoff says,

> in his suffering, or death, or doctrine, or anything
> private or external, taken in itself, but his very per-
> sonality, or what he in the very essence of his being
> *is* in what he thinks, does, and suffers. The reconcili-

13. "De andra tvärtom." Ribbing, *FR*, 122–23.
14. Beside the sensuous and rational, there is, says Boström, no third
being, and consequently there is no third source of knowledge beyond
sense and reason.
15. *SB, 3,* 256–57.
16. *SB, 2,* 494. Boström's views might thus loosely be classified with
liberal as against Scriptural Christianity.

1

ation in its deepest sense is the same as the Redeem-
er, and, therefore eternal; not something past, but
something eternally present. Only the external can
become past. Not so the inner! And the personality
thus leads us from the world of history to that of
eternity.[17]

Boström's general rejection of the religious doctrines of
hell, creation, a fall of man, petitionary prayer, faith, and
sacrifice also have bearing on his relation to Christianity.

Boström's judgments on Christianity result from his
desire to bring about a synthesis between religion and
philosophy under the form of religion as a philosophical
science. It is because he applies his rationalistic system
to Christianity and indeed to all religion with rigor that
he calls some of the elements of Christianity "fantasies."
He wishes to remove from his conceptions of God and
religion everything that from his point of view seems arbitrary and whimsical. The real question in his treatment
of Christianity lies therefore in the validity of his rationalism and absolute idealism. A liberal Christianity
may disagree with Boström over details of his position,
but may sympathize with his approach to the problems
of religion. Biblical orthodoxy, on the other hand, will
question Boström's entire effort, and may challenge his
acceptance of reason over revelation with its consequent
arbitrary use of Scripture and its seeming philosophical
dogmatism.

6. Influence and Evaluation

The third and final volume of Boström's works, edited
by Hans Edfeldt and G. J. Keijser, contains this dedica-
tory page:

17. *BSP*, 111.

To the Memory
of
Our Revered and Beloved Teacher
Christopher Jacob Boström
His Nation's and His Period's Greatest
and most Independent Thinker
This Concluding Collection of His Works
Is now Dedicated
by
The Editors.

Such enthusiastic admiration and devotion indicates that Boström was regarded as a true philosopher by those who knew him most intimately. While it must be evaluated in this setting, there can be no serious question but that Boström made a deep impression on his own nation.

Wikner, in a lecture given at Kristiania, Norway, in 1886, gives something of the background of Boström's influence:

> The idealistic tendency has been preponderant [in Sweden], and it corresponds with the Swedish temperament, which is rather introspective and easily yields to a more or less deep dream-life that is rich in presentiment. . . . This idealism has received its most complete expression in the philosophy of Boström. According to my opinion, this philosophy is a faithful and harmonious reproduction of the Swedish temperament in the form of thought. It has exerted an unprecedented influence, and will long continue to do so in spite of individual protests that are raised against it.[1]

Nyblaeus says that the wish had been expressed in Denmark that the works of Boström could be published

1. *STB*, 11, 13.

there.[2] Höffding gives the information that Denmark had sent a student to Uppsala in 1869 to become familiar with Boström's philosophy.[3] Though he maintains that Boström's influence is already waning (1874), Dons nevertheless admits that it is assured of an extended existence, due to the fact that the leading men in the various professions are his followers.[4]

Anathon Aall, in a comparatively recent book dealing with philosophy in the Scandinavian countries,[5] declares that traces of the influence of Geijer, Grubbe, and Boström can be found even at the present time in the concepts of religion and justice, not only among the educated, but in the general rank and file of the people. He says that their influence has only in part receded.[6] In Aall's book Boström is accorded vastly the major share in the section on Swedish philosophers.[7]

Anders Wedberg, another of the recent writers on Boström, admits that during the second half of the nineteenth century Boström's influence in Sweden was like Hegel's in Germany, so that from 1860 to 1890 Swedish philosophical thought was entirely in Boström's spirit. But he adds that late in that century his influence began to wane. Wedberg makes the assertion that it is not as the founder of a school of philosophy but as the object of criticism that Boström is of the greatest importance in the history of philosophy.[8] He further writes that much of Boström's philosophy now has only idea-and-cultural-historical value, but makes the concession that from some

2. *TUBF*, 1.
3. *FS*, 5–6.
4. *OB*, 8.
5. *Filosofien i norden (FN)*, published in 1919.
6. *FN*, 3, 6.
7. *FN*, 12–42.
8. *LSBF*, 14–15.

points of view Boström's thinking is always worthy of study by the student of the history of philosophy.[9]

Ljunghoff faces the question of Boström's influence in these words:

> There is, finally, the question of the abiding value in Boström's thought. It is not correct to say that all intellectual interest in it is lacking. For even if the aspect of the problem is different now from what it was in Boström's day, it must, nevertheless, be admitted that the fundamental thoughts of his philosophy are in these very days beginning to revive. It is also certain that the one who, though ignorant of Boström, has only a shrug of the shoulder for him does not possess much of the "genuine philosophical spirit and temper that seeks the true and essential in things and strives for its realization and improvement in the world." No doubt there is much in Boström's thought that belongs to the past alone. . . . Modern knowledge does not present a unified picture. It rather reminds us in many ways of the unrest and agitation which in history has always been the harbinger of something new. There is perhaps this difference that the world events that are shaping up[10] at the present have more of the character of world-judgment than at any previous time. It may, however, not be impossible to discern certain fundamental tendencies in the general manner of thinking, and see how from various directions they seem to point especially toward a renewed personal idealism.[11]

9. *LSBF*, 1.
10. This was written during World War I.
11. *BSP*, 117–18.

In 1908 the Boström Society was formed in Sweden. In the Introduction to the first issue of its publication, *Smärre Skrifter,* the editors Karl Pira and G. J. Keijser in a joint article say that Sweden has passed through a period that was inimical to idealism, but that there are signs of a desire to return.[12]

It is thus apparent that Boström had his day of almost complete philosophical influence in Sweden. But it is also apparent that his influence has waned since the beginning of the present century, so that there is no active Boström school in Sweden today. Nor, contrary to Ljunghoff, Pira, and Keijser, has there been any movement toward personal idealism. Whether any followers will want or be able to effect a new Boströmism remains for future years to disclose.

Outside of Sweden, Boström's influence has been negligible. The question arises, therefore, as to his stature in the general stream of Western philosophy. Boström's knowledge of the history of philosophy (which was considerable) made him aware of the fact that in philosophy the field for originality is more limited than in art. He did not, therefore, lay claim to all the originality that his admirers wished to ascribe to him. But he was certain that he had made discoveries that were of the greatest importance. Among these he counted his doctrine that life and self-consciousness are not two separate realities, but are one and the same. He often said that he was the first thinker that had given an answer to the question as to what life is. Boström also believed, as has been already noted, that he was the first philosopher to have investigated the concept of being in its pure generality. It seems certain that he was led to his position by his own reflections on the idea of concrete reality in determinate self-

12. *SS, 1* (1908), 4.

consciousness. From the concrete self-conscious being he presented consciousness as a systematic principle.[13] Thus there may be elements in Boström's thought that indicate original thinking and that may have continuing value and validity. His treatment of religion from an idealistic perspective, his understanding of the psychology of the forms of religious life, his insights into the problems of reason, philosophy, and religion, indeed his general effort to synthesize philosophy and religion in his philosophical science of religion: all these explorations and studies make important contributions and are valuable data for students of philosophy and religion.

In a letter to Nyblaeus in 1861 Boström wrote:

> My philosophy is new, and no one has measured what it contains. I fear that it will die out with me and my nearest disciples. It makes such great demands of the human faculty of thought and on spiritual development in general that only a few will become familiar with it. For that reason I am regarded by the masses as half crazy. But the idealistic philosopher has to be satisfied with this. He understands that it cannot be otherwise. . . . If I do not receive any recognition of my efforts, I can, nevertheless, be satisfied.[14]

One hundred years are a comparatively short time in the history of thought, but they do give some opportunity for perspective. Through this perspective he appears as a man who could think, and who dared to think, independently. To speak of him, as an unknown German writer first did, as the "Plato of the North," may be not merely eulogistic but in fact descriptive of his stature and efforts.

13. Nyblaeus, *TUBF*, 13–16.
14. In Nyblaeus, *FFS, 4*, Part 1, 5–6.

Boström's *Philosophy of Religion*

INTRODUCTION

Religion is not equivalent in meaning to a certain dogmatic manner of representation [dogmatism], or to certain feelings and actions; but it is man's actual rationality,[1] his highest form of life, and highest destiny.[2] Hence religion includes the determinations previously mentioned [dogmatism, feeling, action], but as consequences of the essence of religion. When religion is comprehended in this manner, the philosophy of religion has as its purpose the highest end of man. On this fact its importance depends. One could say that to *have* religion is more important than to *know* it. Religion, however, as a spiritual activity, has no more important ingredient than clear consciousness, which is better than obscurity, and contains greater certainty.[3]

The Greeks, after they had begun to engage in practical philosophy, were concerned chiefly with ethics and politics. With Plato and Aristotle philosophy of religion was the first part of ethics, without the insight that religion is a concept by itself, which is the foundation of ethics and politics. Neo-Platonism indeed began with religion, but was so engaged with the starting point that it did not arrive at the practical use of it as applied to humanity and the state.[4]

It is true that, within Christianity, man early engaged in religious problems, but for a long time rather under

1. "Aktuela förnuftighet."
2. "Högsta bestämmelse."
3. The Cartesian tradition of clear and distinct ideas. See Edfeldt, *Festskrift*, 251.
4. This statement reflects Boström's deep interest in political science. Some of his extensive writings are in this field. See *SB, 1*, 355–416; *2*, 311–476; *3*, 85–163, 330–46.

the form of positive doctrine than as philosophy. When, at the beginning of modern times, one [a philosophy] was really developed, it was at first directed toward the outer world; and when it encountered difficulties with regard to the possibility of knowledge of the outer [world], the chief question for speculation centered around the objectivity of knowledge and man's character and nature as a condition for answering this question.

In the thought of Kant and Fichte, philosophy of religion is still an appendage to ethics. It is only in more recent times that philosophy has been compelled to return to the ultimate principles of the spirit and of nature, even as it has been recognized that religion is indispensable for practical philosophy in its entirety. Thus we have in our own days [1848] witnessed a philosophical point of view which has directed philosophy and religion to each other, although indeed in an improper way, since it has regarded religion simply as a lower form of that which, in a higher form, constitutes philosophy, and comprises its contents.[5]

A protest from the point of view of religion has also arisen against the Hegelian philosophy of religion, and it appears as if the Hegelians have had a foreboding that from this very viewpoint a criticism would arise against the spread of Hegelianism even outside of the school when its adherents sought to validate the fact that there is no medium between either by accepting theology [as]

5. This statement and the following paragraph are directed against Hegel and the Hegelians. It should perhaps be noted that Hegel himself speaks of the reciprocal relations of philosophy and religion rather than as Boström suggests. He says that the content of religion and philosophy is the same, except for details of external nature and finite mind which fall outside the range of religion. Hegel holds that religion should not set herself against comprehending reason and against philosophy in general, especially against a philosophy of which the doctrine is speculation, and so religion. See Hegel, *PM*, 182–83.

4

not to think at all, or else by *opposing* theology. Such a strife between theology and philosophy has arisen once before, namely, when rationalism first arose, when it also revealed the contradictions which the empirical theology included. But thereby the only gain was a spread of religious skepticism and the appearance of Sophists who employed the weapons provided against theology for their own interests. This we must also expect, if we are unable to present something positively satisfactory in religion from a philosophical point of view. Because reason must in all problems be decisive, since it is just what lies outside of reason which is called into question; and from what lies outside of reason no arguments can be produced. Herein lies a special reason now to engage in the philosophy of religion and thereby present a view which, so far as I can see, reconciles philosophy with the Christian consciousness. This also was reasonable, even if more under the form of feeling and imagination.

As a prelude to philosophy one has usually required a phenomenological development as to how one arrives at the previously mentioned principle, in order to assure oneself that this principle is the right one. This is a misunderstanding, because the empirical psychologies swarm with inaccuracies. And to think that one can arrive at philosophy and assure oneself of the rightness of the principle through a reasoning which stems from something else than philosophy, or from some unphilosophical credo, is simply unreasonable. Rather, the principle of philosophy must be such that it can be considered as correct in and of itself, because otherwise it would not be the highest principle.[6] The psychological education that is required for it may be diversified, but the

---

6. Boström holds that philosophy is the science of the principles of the other sciences. See below, p. 9.

means for understanding its principle and for perceiving its truth does not lie in it; this must be accomplished through analysis of the principle itself.

What is the philosophy of religion, and what is its place in the system of philosophy? This question raises two others: What is philosophy? and What is religion? Each of these can be considered from two viewpoints: What is philosophy, and what is religion: (1) in itself? (2) for us? These two must not be confused, but each question must be answered differently. If they are confused, the answer for the one will not be valid for the other.

The question as to what philosophy is in itself can also be expressed by: What is philosophy in its purity and perfection, i.e. without any negations except those which are essential to it? This expression is synonymous with: in itself,[7] because nothing can be more than itself. In like manner the same question finds another expression: What is it in its essence? For the truth and perfection of a thing is its essence in contrast with the phenomena (the manner in which a thing reveals itself to another). Likewise: What is it as to its concept or its idea? Idea is intensification of apprehending or comprehending,[8] just as *percipere* (or perceiving) is of *capere,* namely, *well and securely,* by which [intensification] the apprehending power unites the apprehended with itself, and remains in it as a force. The correctness of what has been said can be seen through reflection on analogous expressions: to penetrate into something, to gain insight into it, etc. Thus idea is clear and distinct, and thereby true perception; such a perception is identical with its

7. From the immediate context it appears that Boström here means "intrinsically."

8. "Omfatta."

6

object.[9] We, therefore, do not seek philosophy outside of ourselves, but in the spirit's own essence or idea.

Again, the latter question, What is *man's* philosophy? does not have the same meaning as the former. [This] is clear from the fact that our philosophy can have many shortcomings [for human experience], which it does not have in itself. Our philosophy is the result of our effort to understand philosophy in itself, and this effort can succeed only relatively, because of our finiteness. Philosophy in itself is related to *our* philosophy as, for example, pure gold to impure. Even the former has certain negative attributes belonging to it—with regard to its weight, etc., added to which, furthermore, there are many others in impure gold, which do not affect it as pure gold.

A preparatory reflection may here be added: Philosophy in itself postulates a similarly perfect subject, whose knowledge it is, since all knowledge must be *someone's.* Because one may well consider it in and for itself and abstract from the knowing subject; but such procedure is only an abstraction, which is true of *all* abstractions, because they all give expression to the subject as seen from a certain point of view. Philosophy, therefore, requires a subject, and if it should reveal itself as infinite, then God alone could be its subject, and then philosophy becomes God himself, seen, namely, as simply knowing.[10] Therefore human philosophy is not the wisdom of the world, but the wisdom of God,[11] because it has God more than the world as object, and the effort is to make

9. Boström's metaphysical monism is found in his repeated statement that nothing originally exists but God and his ideas. Here he also includes epistemological monism.

10. Boström employs several different words for God, as "Gudomlighet," and "Gud." In this translation "God" is used in each instance, since Boström uses them interchangeably.

11. "Världsvishet" and "Gudsvishet."

the content of one's consciousness similar to the content of God's consciousness.

It may, further, be observed that we cannot answer the second question—what philosophy is for man—without first having determined what it is in itself. This seems to imply a contradiction, since *mine* is nearest to me, and it can be questioned whether we can ever arrive at insight of anything else, or anything different. But here it is to be observed that man, as finite, has feelings and representations before he has ideas; consequently he also has faith before he has knowledge. Through the former he acquires a certain acquaintance with the objects; but to gain an idea he must get to the ground of it,[12] whereas, when he wishes to understand by faith and opinion, he does the opposite. Thus [it is] in the present instance. We must begin with what philosophy is in and for us, in order that therefrom we may conclude what it is in itself. On the other hand, we cannot fully *know* the former so long as we *seek* only the latter, just as the phenomenon, as the first with which we are acquainted, gives occasion to seek the being, but can properly be understood only *through* the latter.

Finally, we must here refer to an objection, as follows: "One cannot know what a science is before the end, and everything else is only to make assertions against which others can be counterbalanced." This is trivial or false; the former, if one means the entire content of science; the latter, if the question is simply concerned with a general limitation.

By way of introduction, we may finally be reminded of the fact that the question as to what philosophy is for us can itself be taken in a two-fold sense: What has it been up to the present? The answer here must come from

12. "Gå till följd från grund."

8

the history of philosophy. Secondly: What must it always remain for us? This is what we here have to clarify.

What is *philosophy in itself?* To answer this question, we must proceed from something known, namely, that philosophy is a science, and the highest science. Someone could question the latter. To such a question we should give the answer that, if there is a higher [science], then that is just *the one* we here mean and define. If again it should be asked if there is a higher and a lower science, we would recall the fact that the other sciences assume their principles. Then *one* must exist which is the science of these very principles, and this is then the highest, containing within itself the others *implicite.* As the science that deals with the principles for the other sciences, philosophy is the *ground* for them, and that on which they rest. But ground and sequel (like cause and effect when the question concerns the preceding and the following in time) is one and the same thing, simply more or less developed, when one, as here, is *not* concerned with existence in time. Sequel is part of the ground which in the sequel becomes a part (wherefore a ground can have several sequels). Therefore philosophy, as the ground of the other sciences, includes all that they contain plus something more; that is to say, they are phenomena of philosophy, as the visible sun is of the real sun. If *we* possessed all philosophy, or if our philosophy were philosophy in itself, then no other knowledge would be possible beside this, because it would include everything, except its own negations.

As a science, philosophy is a *knowledge,* and a knowledge *about* something; it has form and content. Form and content are the same, considered more generally and more specifically, namely, as that according to which we answer the questions *how* and *what* the thing is. As a science, philosophy is *formally* determined, (1) as knowing, which again includes, (a) a self-consciousness, the unity itself, and (b) a certain form of it, i.e. a perceiving.

To perceive is to be self-conscious in a determinate way, so that one can answer *how* and *of what* consciousness is conscious. That the word has this meaning can by way of example be illuminated from the ancient scripture, that "the natural man receiveth not the things of the Spirit of God,"[13] i.e. he is not self-conscious to such an extent that he is conscious of them.[14] As to its form, perceiving is: dim, or noticeable only to others; or clear: noticeable to the conscious person himself. The former is feeling; the latter is representation, clearer or more abstract, and more inner, affording a form in space, either of something present, or absent, in which case, however, the perceived is not yet *fully* clear, because the spirit is not in it, but it is for him an object.[15] If a person grasps a portion of the representation with complete clearness, then it becomes idea, which is the highest form of perceiving. Ideas, namely, are certain, and are known as unchangeable, which again coincides with the form of perfection and completeness. *Thus* understood, nothing can be more, or in any other mode, than it is perceived.

Philosophy as knowing is consequently (c) an understanding, but one which is not transition from one perception to another on the level of perceiving. Thus philosophy, as knowledge and science, is a (a) fixed, (b) clear, (c) necessary, and (d) systematic perceiving, because it aims at everything in its object, and thus includes a mani-

13. I Corinthians 2:14.

14. One of Boström's basic words is "förnimma": "to perceive." In this quotation the Swedish has "förnimmer" where the English has "receiveth." The Greek word δέχομαι, which is translated as "förnimmer" and "receiveth," also means "embrace," "make one's own." Perhaps here is a relation to his word, "omfatta." Above, p. 6.

15. "Objectum."

fold, whose moments do not nullify, but postulate each other. Clear perceptions cannot contradict each other. Philosophy is, further, (2) the highest science, (a) qualitatively, i.e. *as science*, fully clear; and (b) quantitatively, the all-embracing, namely, God in his omniscience.[16]

As to its *contents* (determined in a general way),[17] philosophy is the science of that which is in itself, or of the absolutely existing, i.e. of being in a restricted and true[18] sense. It is perfect perceiving. But nothing can be perceived better than as it is in itself, in contrast with the phenomenon, which is the being imperfectly perceived. Since conception is the highest and the perfect form of perceiving; and since the true perception must be a correspondence between the perceived and the absolutely true, i.e. since there must be absolute similarity or identity; or since the perception and the perceived[19] are divided only as *quod* and *quid;* therefore, philosophy, as science of being, becomes the science of concepts or ideas, that is to say, of the absolute reason and its content, which is exactly true being.

Conception, or clear perception, and idea are the same, and there is no difference between the expressions, except that conception more expressively indicates the objective significance, or identity with the existing, than idea, though we have become accustomed to imagining something more pompous with "idea" than is understood by conception, so that idea has almost been lost in something nebulous, wherefore also they who talk a great deal about ideas as a rule are nebulous people. It may, furthermore, be observed that even in the sensuous and

16. Boström here seems to say that philosophy is God. Elsewhere he actually does so.

17. "I allmänhet bestämt."

18. "I inskränkt och egentlig bemärkelse."

19. "Perceptionen och perceptum."

in the empirical sciences we also seek the absolute reason and its content, not immediately, but as referred to *us:* thus, however, the Divine, provided we, as far as regards our essence, are ideas in the absolute reason, and consequently are what constitutes its determination, is apprehended by this reason in and with the apprehension of the idea.[20]

If we now sum up what has been said about philosophy in and for itself, particularly about its form and content, it is apparent that this philosophy is a knowledge which is absolutely independent, which does not require anything else to be complete, since there is nothing beyond the absolute knowledge. Philosophy is, furthermore, an organic whole of ideas, and thus is not sensuous, or divisible, or changeable. It is also a form of life and self-consciousness, namely, the absolute reason with its content, which includes everything in itself. This means that philosophy in itself is (1) not *a* system, but *the* system; (2) yet it is a system, namely, the *infinite* system. If clear concepts are to be found, they must have something in common, namely, in particular that they are measures *(modi)* of self-consciousness and have their unity in this; and when such is the case, they must harmonize with each other, because otherwise they would not be thoughts, according to the principle of contradiction. This system is endless, in positive signification: not what is without limit, but what contains within itself everything that it needs in order to exist, with nothing homogeneous to itself *in addition* to itself. (3) [Philosophy] is knowledge about being, or beings, and hence about reason in its concept. Aristotle already saw that the highest form of thought

20. Beginning with "thus, however," the Swedish is involved: "Således dock det Gudomliga, såvida vi till vårt väsen ock äro ideer hos det absoluta förnuftet och följaktligen vad som utgör dess bestämdhet, fattas av detta förnuft i och med fattandet av idén."

was νόησις νοήσεως; Plato understood the ideas in a similar manner.[21]

The phenomena, on the other hand, are excluded from this philosophy. If someone should ask whether the absolute reason, or God, does not have knowledge of them, the answer must be, Yes, from him no knowledge is excluded, but he knows the phenomena, not as the determinations of *his* consciousness, but of man's. Finally, since no conception is possible without conceiving, and this not without one conceiving, and God's knowing is himself *as* knowing, therefore philosophy in and for itself is God's consciousness of himself; philosophy in itself is God's self-consciousness of himself in the totality of his determinations or ideas, or his life as knowing. If, therefore, philosophy is found in man, it is a participation in God's consciousness and life.[22]

The concept of motion does not belong to the concept of life; what constitutes life in the finite living beings is not motion, but their independence, and this again is found only in self-conscious beings, and the degree of the one is, therefore, equal to that of the other.

Man's philosophy, as is evident from what has previously been said and already intimated, is his consciousness of himself in God and in his system of ideas. Again, it is philosophy in itself with the negations under which it appears in man as a result of his limitations. [Once again] it is the result of the striving to realize himself as

21. The text here is so fragmentary that it is impossible to determine what Boström means. The words are: "Likaså Plato: om ideerna." Literally: "Just as Plato: concerning the ideas." The context seems to indicate that Boström means that for Plato the highest forms of thought were the ideas.

22. That Boström means this in a metaphysical sense is also evident from his statement that man's philosophy is an effort to make the content of one's consciousness similar to the content of God's consciousness. Above, p. 8.

absolutely knowing, or in himself to achieve philosophy in itself; in other words, it is his highest life as a sentient being. Such a philosophy is *possible* for man, provided he is rational, and a participant of the Divine; namely, when he is considered in his truth and essence, i.e. that he is an idea in God, or enters into [God's] knowledge, and that this knowledge—the system of [God's] ideas— is found in the unity of his consciousness, even though more or less clearly.

On the other hand, man's philosophy *differs* from philosophy in itself in the same way as man differs from God: he partakes of [God's] reason—is *rationis particeps* —but *is* not reason. Rational is related to reason as the golden to gold; man indeed grasps all of [God's] ideas, but only a few clearly in each instant of time.[23] Therefore his philosophy also has the same character as philosophy in itself, but only relatively: it is potentially infinite, or has the infinite in itself—as ground—but actually finite (a *pure* negation does not exist); it is more or less organic; is indeed (as to its content) infinite, but only in connection with knowing about something material; and it is eternal, although the knowing develops only in varying ways because of the sensuous and in connection with it. Thus man's philosophy is generally only relatively identical with God's.

The similarity between the two can be greater or smaller, and here the limit cannot be determined in advance. Indeed, it does depend on objective conditions, but also to a degree on the freedom in man himself. Only *this* much is in this instance granted, namely, *that* a difference must be found, even as, on the other hand, it is only relative: wherever there is clarity in the apprehension, there is also philosophical apprehension *of* or *with*

23. "Tidsmoment."

14

respect to the phenomenal world. On this depends the *manner* in which man must proceed to attain philosophy. Much has been said about a method peculiar to philosophy, according to which philosophy should, as it were, follow of itself, or the method coincide with the construction and reality of the object itself. If such a help[24] could be found, it would be very comfortable for philosophizing; but it is not to be found, and is superfluous for the one who can walk by himself. In reality the whole method consists in this: through analysis and abstraction a person goes back to the most simple element in his consciousness, and by means of this he synthesizes the more concrete, in order by synthesis to illuminate the concrete with the clarity he has gained in the more abstract. In this one may indeed find it necessary to skip over certain middle links, and this can lead to a wrong comprehension of them, but it can also lead to a true insight of those intervening moments as determinations of the more concrete which has been *demonstrated from* the principle; in other words, it can lead to a true insight of the middle links which had previously been skipped over, which if all were lacking in the synthetic development itself would make the demonstration in this superfluous. This method has from the beginning of knowledge been the only one, and the correct one; all other arrangement of the order of the conceptions is accidental and immaterial, and an analysis of each conception has always preceded the arrangement of each conception.

Philosophy in itself does not have parts, but is an organic whole. The same kind of knowledge permeates the whole. But man's philosophy permits a division, because man must develop the multiplicity of his determinations in time, or be active, and he can thereby apprehend him-

24. "Ledstol."

self and his world from various points of view, whereby a division arises between theoretical and practical activity. There is for man, as finite, an outer and an inner, and the relation of his activity to these different poles determines the difference in his activity. He can pose as the goal of his efforts the bringing of the obscure to clarity. Under these circumstances he moves from the outer to the inner —which also *per se* is his highest goal. Here he reflects less upon the fact that he is active, although this also enters into his *perceiving*.

There is, furthermore, however, more or less of struggle between the outer and the inner, which calls forth effort to remove this contradiction by *changing* the external to conform to the internal, in which case he reflects less upon the fact that here also there is perceiving. In both instances he seeks harmony, but in the theoretical he seeks it in the things themselves or their being, and in the practical he seeks it in the relation between himself and them. Since man can grasp the essence, or the absolute, only in so far as it is found in him and in his world, his differentiation between the theoretical and the practical activity depends on his differentiation of his philosophy into theoretical and practical activity. In the former the essence, in so far as it is actual in man and in his world is thought of as the ground from which the phenomenal is explained and its contradictions resolved. On the other hand, practical philosophy thinks of the idea or the essence as not yet existing in man and in his world, but rather as that which is only ideally real, which because it is introduced in the phenomena will thereby bring harmony as purpose and law. Only free activity has a purpose. Therefore practical philosophy deals only with it, and thus determines what the activity should be in order to attain the goal.

When we thus divide man's philosophy into theoretical and practical, this is not a division of philosophy itself as such, but only with regard to the point of view from which it conceives its object and its relation to the given. Theoretical philosophy thus deals with the given, which does not depend on man's free activity, but only on the absolute as ground. The practical philosophy does not have anything to do with what is actual in man's world, but with what should *become* actual in it through man's free activity. Thus the one has necessity as object, the other, freedom or *moral* necessity, that is, what is necessary for man as a rational and thinking being, but which in his world is not actual *without* his free activity. The difference between theoretical and practical philosophy can also be expressed in this way: the former deals with the true, the latter with the good. In addition to these, esthetics does not constitute a third part. The beautiful is indeed an object of philosophical observation, but it belongs to the theoretical philosophy.

The theoretical philosophy is divided into: (1) *theology:* concerning the being, or the absolute reason in itself and in its relation to man and his world as the ultimate ground in general, and thereby an explanation of these; (2) *anthropology:* concerning the essence of the individual man, i.e. in a rational being existing in a physical nature; and (3) *ethnology:* with the naturally united man, i.e. a group of individuals as natural—independent of freedom—altogether: the doctrine of tribes, races, and families, as natural societies. The philosophical doctrine of nature does not constitute a special philosophical discipline, but only implies a completion of what is included in the doctrine of man, since nature, as such, exists only in relation to man. Furthermore, the last two divisions of theoretical philosophy may together be called *anthropology* or *cosmology in a broad sense.*

The practical philosophy also includes three parts: this

practical philosophy is the doctrine of reason as purpose and law, whose unity is religion—whence all practical philosophy is the science of religion. This purpose and law can be regarded (1) as such, or for man in general, when it is the *science of religion in a restricted sense;* (2) for the individual man: *ethics* or *moral philosophy;* and (3) for the community or the state, as such, *statecraft* or *political science.* In addition, each part contains the doctrine as to how free human activity should be constituted in order to correspond to its purpose.

The last two divisions of practical philosophy could also be called *jurisprudence*—concerning what is right—in a broad sense.

It may, furthermore, be observed that since the last two divisions in each of the principal parts of philosophy comprise only special applications of the first division of each, therefore according to a strictly systematic order, ethnology should really precede anthropology, and political science precede ethics, in continuing particularizations. But in the successive development of our philosophy we must proceed from the more easily grasped, even though in a strict order of idea-relationships the state, for example, is primary and the individual person exists as an organic part of it.

The correctness of what has just been said about religion and philosophy of religion can easily be seen by the following general remarks, in and by which we also gain the concept of *religion* in itself as man's [religion]. No one can be religious without being rational, and vice versa. If the contrary were true, one could be more or less rational without being religious. Religion would then have no relation to reason, and if such were the case, it could thus not be made man's highest goal, i.e. would not be religion.

The conclusion of this is that a person is religious in

the same degree that he is rational, and vice versa, and that, therefore, religion and reason are identical. Since no one can be more religious or rational than reason, religion in itself is consequently God himself.

Man's religion again stands in the same relation to the absolute religion as his philosophy to philosophy in and for itself. God does not *have* religion, but he *is* religion, and it is wrong to limit its meaning to that of merely human qualification. As thus understood, we can see the importance of religion for man, and to this signification a general one also leads, which lies in the word itself, namely, that man cannot place any higher goal for himself than God. Man's religion has also been called *faith,* which is not the mere conviction, but also a life conforming to it. Here the reason for the name was that from a certain standpoint we do not distinguish between faith and knowledge.

When I say, however, that *religion and reason* in and for themselves are *both God,* this does not mean that they are to be regarded as purely identical, but that in each one we *see God* from a somewhat different point of view. God is the Highest Being with all its determinations; and this we call reason when we think of it only as absolute self-consciousness or perceiving. Religion again is this same reason as binding or determining man's free activity. According to the meaning of the word itself one can trace it from *relegere, religare,* or *colere.* Only man's innermost being can bind him, but then his being is God's.

Therefore man's religion is not something merely theoretical—a manner of representation—but rather something practical; it is willing and doing, even as philosophy of religion is a practical discipline.[25] Every determination in man, even actual knowledge, or consciousness,

25. In this statement lies an explanation of the general character of Boström's *Philosophy of Religion.*

is immediately united with practical activity, or the results of it. Man's life is a continuous activity in time, and, therefore *his* original nature is to be active practically, i.e. to be *will*. The will determines the end, and directs the activity toward it.

The correctness of the division of philosophy which has been presented gains confirmation by giving attention to the manner in which philosophy has shaped itself historically, in which no other division has been satisfactory, except the one now made by me.[26] In the *Orient* there is no *philosophy;*[27] it is related to Europe as fancy to reason, but without organization.

The Greeks were the first to develop philosophy with a certain organization. At the beginning it was merely theoretical philosophy without divisions, such as, cosmology, anthropology, theology, because the external and the internal fused. Toward the end of the first period, however, a two-fold reality was distinguished, as also a two-fold science: the one concerning being, or theology, and the other an empirical science, physics. Plato accepted this division, and added a third, ethics, which was first developed by the Sophists and Socrates. The ethics of Socrates was also statecraft, both in one, because among the Greeks there was no state, but only communities. With Socrates, therefore, as with the Greeks generally, the entire practical philosophy became ethics, whereof the science of religion merely became a part, and politics a major part.

Aristotle took a forward step in the organization, using the same three-fold division. With him, however, there

26. This observation reflects Boström's implicit confidence that he had presented a new and unimpeachable philosophical system.

27. This statement seems extreme in view of the fact that Boström accepted some of Oriental thought, as, for instance, transmigration. The explanation here may be in Boström's view that Oriental thought was not critical enough. See below, pp. 46–47, 54, 79.

is another, in accordance with the division of human activity: the theoretical and the practical. Thus he also divided philosophy into theoretical and practical. But in Aristotle's philosophy the economy[28] is not a philosophical consideration, and ethics and politics fall together. The subsequent Greek philosophers retained the threefold division, but the first division with them became only a formal part—as a residuum of Aristotle's logic—which is only a part of anthropology. Neo-Platonism was without organization because of Oriental influence. It contained only theology and philosophy of religion.

At the beginning of modern times there was only imperfect organization. Bacon divided [philosophy] according to imagination,[29] memory, and reason; but his philosophy is only empirical. Wolff was the first to divide philosophy into theoretical and practical, the former (the theoretical) into logic and metaphysics, and metaphysics into ontology, cosmology, psychology, and theology; and the practical into ethics and natural law, politics, and international law. But in opposition to this it is to be observed that (a) logic is not a chief part of philosophy, but a part of anthropology; (b) metaphysics does not have ontology as a special part, because it contains only what is common in the other three parts, and therefore in reality only these other three parts; (c) if it is true (as Kant showed) that the cosmos is only a phenomenon, then the science of it is not a special philosophical discipline; thus the parts of theoretical philosophy that I have designated remain, except that ethnology had not yet arisen; (d) practical philosophy embraced only ethics and natural law—politics became the public natural law; wherefore it happens that accepting natural law as a part

28. "Ekonomiken."
29. "Fantasi."

of philosophy rests on a misunderstanding. It is only politics, for otherwise it would be one with ethics, because reason cannot make laws for a man in a condition in which it forbids him to remain.

Kant has made his division in transcendental philosophy, which investigates the cognitive faculties, divided into the different critiques, and metaphysics, the theoretical dealing with nature, and the practical dealing with morals. This is an unfortunate division, because according to Kant, nature is itself a phenomenon and, therefore, belongs to anthropology. The practical philosophy is incomplete, because practical philosophy also has to do with the law; the transcendental is not philosophy, but must precede it, and is therefore only metaphysics with a theoretical though unorganized part, and a practical part, namely, ethics and natural law. Fichte also has only a theoretical and a practical part, and the former only anthropology, the latter ethics and natural law.

Hegel has made a new division. Nature and spirit are equally real and, therefore, his philosophy has become a philosophy of nature and spirit, in which both have something in common. But while with Schelling this became empty in content—the abstract identity between nature and spirit, or a negation of both—Hegel, on the other hand, presented logic as the common general form or concept of nature and spirit, in the sense of a metaphysical science (just as the dialectic in Plato).

This three-fold division by Hegel is neither like that of the Greeks, nor an improvement of it, nor can it be justified in the system. Logic, which is supposed to contain the general forms of thought, and is related to the rest as general grammar is to the special languages, does not in this way have any special content. Plato's dialectic did have it, because its object, the Ideas, did not need the other parts of philosophy, although, on the contrary, with these it was also theology.[30] Hegel's physics is not similar to Plato's physics, because the latter refers only to the sensuous existence; this however, completely understood, also includes man as phenomenon.

Hegel also assigns man's sensuousness to the philosophy of spirit, but considers that of the animals under natural philosophy, though there is no difference in nature between them. Ethics in Hegel is only a physics, because it does not consider what ought to be done, but morality is regarded as that which has become reality. Moral philosophy thus becomes equivalent to the history of philosophy and, therefore, not practical, as if only a plus or a minus of ideality is the difference between nature and spirit. Here, then, a difficulty appears in the system itself, namely, that nature and spirit comprise thesis and antithesis, whence logic does not become thesis; but the parts of philosophy become, *first*, the philosophy of nature, *then* of the spirit, and for the *third*, logic. Finally, the philosophy of spirit includes the doctrine of the subjective, the objective, and the absolute spirit. But such a philosophy is not found in the Hegelian system. According to Hegel's system, spirit is the inner[31] side of nature, and does not exist without it.[32] The content of the doctrine of absolute spirit, therefore, becomes: art,

30. "Ehuruväl tvärtom med dessa, den var alltså teologi."
31. "Den inre sidan."
32. Boström's observation here does not seem to harmonize with Hegel's words: "From our point of view Mind (or Spirit) has for *presupposition* Nature, of which it is the truth, and for that reason its *absolute prius*. In this its truth Nature is vanished, and mind has resulted as the 'Idea' entered on possession of itself. Here the subject and object of the Idea are one—either is the intelligent unity, the notion. This identity is *absolute negativity*—for whereas in Nature the intelligent unity has its objectivity perfect but externalized, this self-externalization has been nullified and the unity in that way been made one and the same with itself. Thus at the same time it *is* this identity only so far as it is a return out of nature." *PM*, 6.

religion, and philosophy. But art is always a product of the human spirit, and, therefore, not absolute. Religion is regarded only as historical or mythological, whereas religion has a much wider signification, to which its imperfect form does not belong, but to man. With us philosophy is merely knowing alone, *without* also being will.

Philosophy of religion, as a new, separate, and practical division of philosophy, is concerned with religion for man, or man's religion. The science of religion in itself, as is evident from its meaning as previously mentioned, belongs to *theology*.[33] As such, it must first present the human religion, or the religious state of mind, in its purity, with conviction, and with beauty; it must also present the immediate products of it, as well as man's hopes united with it; and this is the true philosophy of religion. Besides this, it must likewise account for religion in the limitations and frailties with which it appears in time in mankind, such as sin or false and imperfect religion. It must also account for the way in which man is brought back to religion, i.e. salvation and improvement. It must also provide the means for it —the church and revelation.

Finally, the history of religion may also be subjected to a philosophical observation, namely, how the idea of religion has successively appeared and the reasons for the order of development. Before philosophy of religion, and as a necessary introduction to it, we must, however, give a presentation of theology and anthropology—just as theoretic conviction is itself a moment in religion, and the religious conviction should indeed be the fully correct theology. The doctrine of freedom prepares the transition from the theoretical propaedeutics to the true practical science of religion.

33. Above, p. 17.

One could ask about the importance of, and the interest in, philosophy of religion. Here it may be remarked that, strictly speaking, it is improper to talk about the importance of that which has worth in and for itself. And, by way of information, it may also be mentioned that a thing has interest for a person in so far as it enters, as a moment, into his innermost being, or has a necessary relationship to it.

Spinoza says that all that man strives for is good, but not, on the contrary, that he strives for something because it is good; and this remark, properly understood, is true. As to his essence, man is a force, and the nature of such a force is not to work for something exterior, but according to its own nature; and in the measure that something stands in relation to it, it becomes a good for the active individual. Thus, for example, the object of a sensuous desire is a good when it is sought, although it can be an evil in relation to man's total tendency, according to which all without exception is measured.

But just *that* is religion, which, therefore, has absolute value and interest; everything else is a consequence of its relation to it. In this value and interest philosophy of religion has a part. It is not religion itself, but an activity which seeks to bring religion to clarity, and thereby also man in his religion to freedom, both in relation to God and to other people. Because that which is clear to him is also something inner and his very own, and not merely an external.

The meaning of philosophy of religion for the practical philosophy has already been touched. Without a correct philosophy of religion ethics and politics are impossible. It is important, finally, for life to be able to retain the purely rational and free in religion without mingling it with anything sensuous which, especially in times of religious unrest, so often happens when expressions of sensuous instincts and desires are assumed, and people believe that they can further religion with them, as for example, persecutions.

With the possession of philosophy of religion it is possible calmly to observe, judge, and measure the worth of the positive religions, without discarding everything in them, because certain elements in them have the significance of a covering for the truly religious.[34]

A positive religion arises in the same way as the individual himself in his various degrees of development, i.e. his different ways of thinking and acting. Usually a certain religious consciousness appears in *one* person, and since this consciousness is an expression of the age in which he lives, it is accepted by the rest. In the founder of the religion, however, all of *this* religious consciousness is found, and all subsequent development of *that* religion simply becomes a growth in the comprehension or presentation of what already existed in the founder. When the cult has been established, and the teachings of the founder collected, the need arises to build them into a unity, so that the scattered doctrines of the founder are apprehended under certain rubrics and in certain statements, which are supported by the authority of the founder, and also not found to be internally inconsistent.[35]

These positive religious doctrines thus arise in the same way as the positive systems of jurisprudence: through the repetition of similar procedure, according to the sense of right, in several similar instances, this procedure is determined to constitute law, and the laws

34. Boström believed that he presented philosophy of religion from the Christian standpoint. It is presumable that he was especially concerned with the form of Christianity in which he was brought up. See below, p. 27.

35. "I strid med sitt eget inre."

are then assembled and arranged into an empirical system.

Later the philosophic sciences of religion arise. When several churches, or different authorities in the same church, arise, a reconciliation of those engaged in the strife can naturally not be from these themselves, because they all constitute, or base themselves on, historical-empirical authority. For the settlement of the struggle we must, rather, seek a higher principle. Thus it was in Greece at the time of the Sophists; thus also at the Reformation. *This* is the meaning of the philosophic science of religion: it is an attempt to determine religion by reason.

The purpose and function of the philosophic science of religion is, therefore, not necessarily to war against the positive religious doctrines. On the other hand, a dispute can arise as to whether the standpoint of the philosophical science of religion is higher than that of the positive, or lower. This can be true with regard to philosophical views at variance with Christianity, which have been such as have developed out of lower principles than Christianity. On the other hand, a philosophy which has attained the highest principle cannot easily come into conflict with Christianity, except in that which for religion itself is immaterial.

A philosopher cannot readily get away from the religion into which he was born, except as to what concerns the non-essential in it. He may possibly give another explanation of the content of the positive religious doctrines, as Copernicus did about the motion of the heavenly bodies, but thereby the positive still remains with *its* worth. So far as religion is concerned, therefore, we do not need to be afraid of the development of philosophy, but we only need to turn polemically against what from a lower view than that of religion wishes to establish itself as philosophy.

The question may be asked as to how, since philosophy has arisen, we can be assured that it will not annul positive religion. It can be done only through insight as to their relationship, as essence and phenomenon, in which case no annulment can come into question. But *this* must be acknowledged, that in a battle within the positive religious teaching the rational must be the norm for the decision. Correspondence with the empirical religious doctrine may be taken as an indication of the perfection in principle of the rational, so that it is doubtful that the latter discards any of the leading features in the positive. Should it, however, become apparent that this must be done, then it is patently unreasonable that the one who has seen something clearly should abandon it because of external compulsion.

But, some one may say, the rational science of religion can proceed from false principles, and is variable. Indeed, but it is the same way with the positive religious doctrine as soon as it develops into a system. In any case it is clear that, if a rational system offends anyone's feelings, he will not accept it.

The one who is to study philosophy of religion must have interest in religion and the higher life of man. This implies that this life in some measure already is real in him, because the one who feels the need of instruction already has some knowledge. This study also posits a need to gain clarity as to one's position[36] with relation to the whole more than to any special part of it. Such a study, therefore, is not for all, but nature itself has divided the aptitudes and talents.[37] But this much can be required of each one, namely, that he may have a view of the whole, and thus see himself, in his branch, as a part of

36. "Bestämdhet."

37. In a controversy with Borelius, Boström says of him that he was not intended by our Lord to be a thinker. *SB, 3,* 181.

the whole. The one who gives himself chiefly to philosophy of religion has thereby indeed also chosen a branch, but the chief one. In addition, acumen and depth are needed, as well as the power of independent research. Through an apprehension only of what others have taught, one receives a lower and merely historical viewpoint.

CHAPTER I

[RELIGION IN GENERAL]

THE MEANING OF RELIGION—in itself and as man's religion—we have already clarified in the introduction to these lectures, and have considered it further in the teaching concerning God's metaphysical attributes.[1] In this teaching we have also presented the [doctrine] of religion in itself, inasmuch as this is God himself in a certain relation to man. The true philosophy of religion, on the other hand, as essentially practical, is, as to its content and object, a doctrine concerning religion as it exists in and for man; or, in other words, it is the doctrine concerning the religious man.

Here we only add a few clarifying remarks to what has been said about religion in general. One can ask: How can one distinguish between man's religion in itself, and for man? [We can do it] for the reason that, when we speak of man, we can mean man as he is in his present temporal state[2] or life; then we think of him from a religious point of view. When we think of the religious man, we have to consider his human religion. Or [we can think of] man as an idea in God, or man as he is, not *actu* in a certain period of time for himself, but for God; and thus, from a religious point of view, [we can] consider his divine religion.

Furthermore: How can God be active in the finite being?[3] God is the ground of the finite being, since nothing

1. Boström refers to his views of God as developed in his theology. See Ribbing (ed.), *FE*, 115-31, and also below, Appendix, par. 58-65.

2. "Tidsmoment."

3. In the original this part is a continuation of the previous paragraph. Since the paragraphs are usually lengthy, the liberty is taken of breaking them up into shorter ones.

exists except life, which, therefore, as such, or as to its general nature, is included in everything; an outside and inside does not exist in the spiritual, but only an existence in each other.[4] That which is in itself unchangeable can indeed be active in something else, if this stands in such a relation to it that the former is a force, i.e. operates in it. Thus, for example, with the power of repulsion of things upon others without any change in the repelling. God acts upon man by being the ground of his life and activity, because the last in time, or that *into which* the activity develops itself, becomes the ground in an *active* life; ground, therefore, has here the meaning of end and law, i.e. the end in each moment of the developing series.

To what does God lead man? To himself, i.e. to rationality as actual in him [man]; or he gives [man] the power of self-determination to the same end, or to become a guiding unity for all the forces subordinated under his unity; that is to say, he gives man reason's *form, content,* and *life*—all of this in so far as it is possible for man because of his limitations; or he gives him power [to enjoy] the beautiful, the true, and the good. But [he leads man] to something even still greater, since religion gives man power to determine himself for this end, namely: he leads him to holiness and righteousness; or to wisdom, goodness, and perfection; although, due to man's finiteness, this can occur in each moment of time only to a certain degree.

Here, then, we have the meaning of man's religion as human or, what is the same, of the religious man. It is man himself, provided he is a participant in the absolute religion, thus with the same end, but in a lower sphere. In this he is himself the leader, although led by the Divine, that is to say, by freely accepting[5] this [guidance].

4. A difficult expression: "blott ett i hvartannat vara."
5. "Ett fritt upptagande."

That man himself thus guides,[6] though guided, is no contradiction, but means that he, though guiding, is regarded, and stands, under a still higher principle, just as the state guides all its members, but just thereby, as itself not absolute, itself is guided by a higher principle; and likewise as the citizens of a state, if they absorb the spirit of the state, thereafter themselves control their environment.

6. "Styra."

CHAPTER II

THE HUMAN[1] RELIGION AND
THE RELIGIOUS ACTIVITY
CONSIDERED IN ITS UNITY:
AS THE WORSHIP OF GOD

BY WAY OF INTRODUCTION to the presentation of
the philosophy of religion, it is necessary that we rid ourselves of some common elements of one-sidedness[2] with
regard to the meaning of religion in and for man, in
order that we thereupon may proceed to the consideration of the activity in and with which the religious life
as such immediately appears.

Religion in man is man himself as a unity in all his
multiplicity;[3] accordingly, religion also becomes such a
unity in and for all the moments[4] in man. It is this, however, not simply as an abstract unity or identity in all
the moments, but as a unity which develops itself into
multiplicity, and then again reveals itself as the unity
in and *by* it. Religion does not have any special relationship to certain human faculties, but rather stands in antithesis to them all as a regulating unity and passes over
into all of man's powers as a unity and all-ness[5] present
in them, and thus becomes man himself as present in all
his functions.

From this it can be seen that religion is not merely

1. "Mänskliga."
2. "Ensidigheter."
3. "Mångfald."
4. "Momenter."
5. "Allhet." This is apparently a word that Boström coined. It conveys the idea of inclusiveness.

feeling, as Jacobi and Schleiermacher defined it. The former said that religion is merely feeling of God, and faith founded on this feeling, which did not admit of any evidence. This, however, would make religion merely subjective and an *actus* without content, whereby religion closes itself against all elucidation. But since the understanding requires clarity, the Jacobian contention is properly to be understood in such a manner that, though religion also is *feeling*, it is not *only* that.

Schleiermacher defined religion as an absolute feeling of man's absolute dependence on God. But, no matter how absolute the feeling may be, it is never identical with God himself, provided one does not wish to make him into simply an abstract unity. An absolute feeling is, furthermore, a contradiction, and: religion does not go out of itself in order to determine the multiple as something beside itself, or as something upon which it exercised no power.

Another—the contrary extreme—is Hegel's insistence that religion is only the power of the general[6] in man, or simply knowing and willing: religion would then be the objective, or with its object, identical, knowing, or ethical conduct according to *general* maxims. But religion is found in man even when he has not risen to this stage of development; it is in the time-process first and predominantly feeling, and never ceases also to be feeling; it is, therefore, just as well a form of knowing and willing, as also of feeling and struggle. If religion, therefore, is not merely feeling, but also not merely a knowing and a willing, but the one as well as the other, as a unity of them all, then it includes all the human functions, or comprises them in their harmonious development for man's highest end.

6. "Det generalas makt."

34

The form of activity which is directly religious is the *cult,* or the worship of God, by which is understood neither the merely theoretical or the merely practical activity in man, which immediately tends toward the *general* realization of religion in him, or the incorporation of the Divine in his consciousness and the subordination under it of his activity. It must be distinguished from all other functions, which deal with something special, although it is not without influence on them. [It is] like the activity of the citizen, which consists in making himself conscious of the meaning and importance of the community, in order to stir up his consciousness about them, or to incorporate them in his consciousness and gain the power of the community spirit in relation to, or as determining in, all his other activity.

This religious activity can be partly private, by the individual, partly public, in connection with [the activity] of others, as the citizen strengthens the community spirit not only in himself, but also in others. Thus one has to distinguish between an individual and a public cult; both need to be united, because the individual reaches completeness principally in the congregation. The combined cult can, moreover, appear in various circles, as in the family, or the community—*par préférence* as a result of the possibility of its members coming together; nevertheless, [it can] also [appear] in the state through common festive days.

The moments in the purpose of the cult are: the *elevation* of the human spirit to God, and inspiration by God; also *subordination* or submission under an ovation in and of the Divine, or: elevation to God; devotion and submission, or piety (as *one* virtue or expression of the religious manner of thinking, not as all of this); and peace and joy in God. The elevation and the devotion differ from each other only as the beginning and the conclusion

35

of the same ceremony:[7] to raise man to the immaterial—or a partial victory over the evil, not triumph, which is the total annihilation of the enemy—of which devotion is the result. Devotion *can* be called enthusiasm; this word, however, like *Begeisterung,* really only indicates the theoretical in connection with it; devotion is man's entire being completely filled by God. Piety is the state of mind in which one freely subordinates one's activity to the demands on it which lie in religion. It is always a constraint, namely, of sensuousness, but not as a loss of freedom, but quite the contrary: man's power is heightened through piety, and it is just this state of mind, to feel oneself more perfect, which is the other side of piety —just as the case is with the citizen who feels *his* purpose to be gained because he realizes or works for that of the state.

It is these two sides in goodness or piety which are designated by submission and ovation, just as it [piety] as a whole is the more practical side in the purpose of the cult, as over against devotion as the more theoretical.

After indicating the purposes of the cult the question becomes the one as to the means through which these shall be attained: the acts which we call religious adoration, and which can be several and of different kinds, according to varying stages of development. The lowest form of it (for the feeling) is the collecting of the feeling away from the external, which is gained through quiet, wherefore the service begins with it. Of similar significance are such symbolic acts as, for example, the folding of the hands: external rest. Here, further, the religious music belongs, with another character than that of the esthetic: not a definite presentation of a certain idea of art, but of the religious feeling in general; wherefore the

7. "Akt."

melody in it is lowly in order not to elicit particular fancies, and more indefinite, whereas the harmony is preponderant. Likewise [it is] with other esthetic meditations: a beautiful day, etc.

Thereupon the collected spirit breaks forth in prayer and song, expressions partly of the majesty of God, and partly of man's insignificance, which already are higher than the mere feeling and achieve results on man's higher theoretical capacities. Here the highest consists of meditations and admonitions which not only have a theoretical purpose, but also a practical and an esthetic one. From the purpose of the prayer it follows that it is not a petition but an adoration in general; it does not enter in upon anything special but upon that which is general; if it moves to something special, then it has lost its religious purpose, and one does not then receive that for which one prays, because one prays amiss. The prayer may indeed be concerned with numerous individual interests, especially the higher ones, but only for the purpose of achieving a certain breadth, not to receive something in particular or everything as such, but only in general to lift man to God. The same is also true about the song, which chiefly occurs in the public cult, while on the other hand the individual engages in quiet meditation. The prayer must therefore not be wordy.

The third form of the adoration is the religious meditation or, as public, the address. Concerning this it is true that its purpose shall not be exclusively theoretical, practical, or esthetic, but man's general elevation to God, from which it can be seen that a religious address must not be a scientific treatise as evidence or elucidation of knowledge concerning a certain object; it does indeed strive for the truth, but not necessarily clearness in detail, and proofs cannot and should not be presented, because what is said may be considered as evident, and the purpose is to elicit fantasy and reason to a spirited occupation with the subject. It should close with this aspect, as it began with the more theoretical consideration. Finally, it should not be an esthetic work of art, aimed only at satisfying the esthetic sense, but only to the extent that it does not offend it. In a word, its purpose is to awaken, admonish, and edify in general.

The second purpose of the cult, namely, piety, is gained through the acts which we call religious sacrifice,[8] or the voluntary offering to God, and has as its object giving to man the tendency of mind[9] whereby he subordinates his purpose under God. These activities can also act preponderantly on feeling, on fantasy, and on reason and the corresponding faculties. The acts are symbols, but they serve to strengthen the tendency just mentioned.

The first acts are those of homage to God (for example, bowing the knee), by which is understood that their purpose is simply to give physical expression to the necessity of subordinating ourselves under God. We have further, as higher moments, thanksgiving and praise (which correspond to prayer). Thanksgiving is a surrendering of egoism to the one from whom one has received a good. Such acts do not have in view[10] receiving further blessings. Finally, there is sacrifice, not necessarily in the old sense of something special, but acts which imply a restraint on the demands of sensuousness, and an increase of the spiritual life. The festivities among the ancients had as their aim costly outlays,[11] which were dedicated to God. This, however, is not necessary, but they do imply the unity of submission and ovation, or the consciousness of the fact that the sacrifices signify an absolute gain.

8. "Sakrifikation."
9. "Riktning."
10. "Åsyfta."
11. "Kostnader."

What remains is to indicate how the cult should be organized appropriately as public, which can be done in numerous ways. The general rules for it follow from what has already been said. Certain individuals must represent the congregation, since the cult is to be performed by several.[12] The reason for this is that it should have in view both purposes mentioned, in such a way, however, that the first precedes and is preponderant in the former part, and the second in the second part. The spiritual address [sermon] constitutes the central part, after which there are prayers, which assume the character of ovation, with which symbolic offerings are united. This, however, more properly belongs to the doctrine of the church. On the other hand, the individual cult cannot be determined according to certain rules.

A remark ought to be made here. In Swedish, cult is called divine worship,[13] for which divine service[14] is not quite proper.[15] This word is an expression of the standpoint of the religious consciousness, when man places God and himself in sharp contrast with each other, as Lord and servant, and devotes a part of his activity to him, and the rest to himself. But God does not gain anything through his activity. In that case one should rather call all of life a divine service.

Hitherto we have spoken about religion as unity, and about the fact that the activity through which it appears as such is inner, and touches all human power, but only

12. It seems evident that Boström is here speaking particularly of the Church of Sweden.

13. "Gudsdyrkan."

14. "Gudstjänst."

15. The Swedish word "kult" is given in English as "cult." *The New Century Dictionary* gives "worship" as one meaning of "cult," but says that it is obsolete. Since Boström gave his lectures in 1844–49, it may be assumed that he means "worship." Above, p. 35.

brings them to a head,[16] or gives them an impulse. For that reason, religion may appear as poor in content. But the richness of its content will become apparent as we proceed to the next chapter.[17]

16. "Går blott till deras spets."

17. Boström ends this chapter with the words, "när man övergår till betraktande av," without a period, thus leading directly into the caption of the next chapter. But it seems better in this translation to conclude as above.

CHAPTER III

THE HUMAN RELIGION OR
THE RELIGIOUS MAN
IN HIS STATES

1. The Religious Man's Relation to Deity

WE KNOW that man is an idea in God, in which case[1] he [God] is and is considered center and subject; but [we also know] that man can be considered as subject for himself, as a rational being, and as such relatively identical with, and relatively opposed to[2] God, and that as such a being he can approach relative unity with his idea.[3] His relation as religious is here that between a guiding principle and himself as guided by it; not, however, without independence, but as a condition withal of being guided by himself, or himself guiding,[4] *by means of*[5] the guiding Being; these two sides, however, of the religious man's relation to God appear somewhat different at different levels of religious culture. At the beginning of this [culture] the former side is preponderant, so that a person is more in the position of being guided; or, religion has him; but in due time he has religion, and by means of it he guides himself. This is the correct [situation], a condition of being guided and self-guiding, and is conceivable when man's essence is the divine idea, and when he becomes more independent, the more he realizes himself,[6] so that the religious situation becomes

---

1. "Varvid."
2. "Relativt motsatt."
3. This is a recurring emphasis in Boström.
4. Above, p. 32.
5. "Genom."
6. "Ju mer hon blir till för sig själv."

one of cooperation (not merely interaction) in the sense that, without God, the religious life would not be possible.

If we consider this condition more closely with regard to man as self-consciousness and activity, then religion, with regard to the former, is a revelation of God for himself—not revelation to him through certain organs for its communication, but the relationship between God and man by which all more special revelations become possible; God *permits* him to behold his essence, but *he* beholds it, and in that case as his own essence. From a practical point of view it becomes the relationship of guiding and being guided, or of absolute dependence and freedom, which do not contradict each other, since man's true essence in fact is the divine. He cannot change his principle, if he wishes to be religious, but neither does he have any desire to do so, inasmuch as it is by free determination. The religious man is ethical by free choice, and vice versa.

2. The Religious Man's Relation to Himself

Since we know that religion includes knowing God, man, and the relation of both to each other, the first thing that man as religious discovers is that God is the ground of his powers. From this fact comes the conviction that these are given to him for the purpose that God has determined, whereby the powers receive a higher meaning than merely that they are his own or nature's—a point of view above which he should rise. The conception of his powers hereby indicated, which is true of them all, including the sensuous, even though the divine appears more in the higher than in the lower, is a moment in the religious manner of thinking. Thereby they are all hallowed in the consciousness, and thus become moments in the service of religion.

But man's knowledge of God must also occasion an activity in him [man], and stand out as determining this [activity], so that it shows that his powers have been given for the highest purpose, and become laws for them, so that a person may not use them as he pleases, and that the laws according to which he uses them are divine and holy. His religion thus becomes an effort to give his powers a direction toward God as the highest center, so that both the science (in all its moments), and morality, receive the character of something holy, or of godly life in man; or such a character that through his knowledge and his activity he partakes in the divine life.[1] This may indeed be done from a certain position in the whole, but, nevertheless, in such a way that even when a person devotes himself to a certain science or activity, these become moments in the whole. Only he who cultivates his science as a link in the whole, pursues it properly and religiously. Likewise, if a person correctly understands his life's calling, no matter what it may be, he will regard it as a moment of the religious activity. In this manner religion will theoretically achieve the result that it will strengthen a person's certainty about, and faith in, the truth, and will produce the insight that, even though doubt may be a starting point as to knowledge, it can, just as little as criticism, be its highest end, because God is that which is certain in itself.

In the moral activity religion appears as faith in the possibility of the good, and gives man power to labor for it. The religious person can, of course, see that a certain end is not always attained, and may even admit that a whole period with regard to religion can be desperate enough; but never does he lose the conviction that man in general and God will attain their purpose. Finally, as

---

1. For Boström's position on freedom, see below, pp. 68–69, 169.

to the esthetic intuition and production, religion has the effect of giving it a religious distinctness, so that it eliminates[2] the coarse in art, and this is placed in a proper relationship to religion.

After having considered the relation of religion to the human powers in general, we must, further, make a survey of its influence on the special human capacities and their manifestations. Its general effect on the sensuous [capacities] is that they become means for the religious [capacities], not in such a way that they are used arbitrarily, or are destroyed, but so that they themselves go in as moments in man's purpose. [This is true] even if alone [the capacities] cannot fill his life, because the religious person develops them in the service of religion.

So far as man's rational powers are concerned, they are in themselves radically[3] religious. They are theoretical, practical, and esthetic. The lowest expression, as to its form, of the theoretically rational capacity is feeling, and of the practical, love. So far as the esthetic [capacities] go, we concern ourselves less with them, because they are only a certain activity of the theoretical and the practical. From the rational standpoint, feeling is never unconscious, be it as pleasure or discomfort, but, moreover, very soon[4] it appears as consciousness of something objective, because the rational feeling appears later than the sensuous, since man, as sensuous, already has an object before himself. Religion then arouses a feeling of respect for a being on whom man knows himself in some way to depend—though in *what* way is not clear—and of humility with regard to himself.

This is its [i.e. religion's] highest form; at the first it appears as a feeling of fear and powerlessness, in a servile

2. "Avstryker."
3. "Till sin rot."
4. "Redan tidigt."

44

turn of mind, because God is thereby not grasped as personal being, but as original reality[5] and original substance,[6] which man places outside of himself, either as a part of the whole, or as the earth, heaven, etc. This form is a consequence of the fact that man's inner being[7] is slightly developed; and since he himself is sensuous, he feels himself to be dependent on the sensuous, and inferior to it in power. It is only when man has apprehended himself as a person that God also becomes a person for him, at first grasped under finite anthropomorphisms, both in a lower and a higher signification.

The feeling also follows to the second standpoint of religious consciousness, at which fear is modified into respect and reverence in the human sense, and then appears in the highest degree of development of this consciousness as pure and disinterested reverence and love, as well as humility: the same, whether referred to God or man.

From a practical point of view, these forms just mentioned correspond to, first, involuntary obedience—due to the fact that man does not seek to approach God, and yet cannot escape him. From this comes the religious activity, which seeks to appease God, and to gain favor with him.[8] This has little influence on his practical activity in general, except to the extent that he abstains from certain deeds which are displeasing to God, and gives gifts to him. On the other hand, from the highest standpoint of the religious consciousness, the practical becomes a voluntary love to God, because from this standpoint man does not consider himself and God to be in a hostile or external relation to each other, and

5. "Urrealitet."
6. "Ursubstans."
7. "Det inre för människan."
8. "Ställa sig in hos honom."

[considers] himself in his unity with God. In this form the religious activity appears in connection with the voluntary morality.

On the power of imagination, and the practical activity that results from it, religion works in such a manner that it sets the power of imagination in motion in order to form a certain way of representation concerning God and man's relation to him, as, for instance, mythical figures. In a practical way, this impels to certain acts, which are determined by these representations. From this standpoint *natural religion* stands lowest, in which God is thought of as merely reality, in many forms, as, certain earthy objects, fetishism, the heavenly bodies, or heaven itself. Finally, through a kind of reflection on God as *the unity,* by abstraction from all special determinations, he is thought of simply as primary substance, who transforms himself into the finite beings as a kind of apparition[9] of him (so *in specie*[10] in Buddhism), which is pantheistic religion in the real sense.

All of these forms appear, since man has not yet comprehended himself, and the feeling of the infinite is preponderant in him. They belong chiefly to Asia. They indicate a progression in religious consciousness in which religion gives them their meaning. In all mythological religion we must, namely, distinguish two moments: that which is itself religious, which forms the unity and can continually remain identical; and the manner of its execution, which can vary, although it also reacts on the comprehension of the principle.[11] In the Orient, where the religious consciousness is stronger, the images reveal a tendency toward infinity, or pantheism, and become

9. "Fantasmata."

10. Boström uses the expression *in specie* several times. It appears that he uses it in a figurative sense, "as to the idea," or "as to the notion."

11. "Verkar tillbaka på principens uppfattning."

arbitrary and more allegorical, since God cannot be *seen* in nature, but this rather becomes make-believe.[12]

Then religion exists under the form of belief and feeling, which uncritically supplies material for the manner of representation, and the certainty that the religious feeling possesses is transferred to the myth. Usage[13] is thereby directed more upon the religious in general, rather than having influence on life; a certain complex of actions is determined by religion, and thus becomes religious, but the rest continue without regard to religion; wherefore it does not determine all actions, but only a few, for example, those touching family, cult, etc.

But when man develops himself into a consciousness of himself as a person, then the mystical religion also develops into its second form, as *anthropomorphic,* and thereby actually into a more divine [religion]. The transition itself to this form constitutes the anthropomorphizing of pantheism: God is *one* being who, as it were, represents the whole world, but as a human being (or man), who is present *in* his world; thus it was in Persia (the personification of light), just as our ancestors did from the beginning.

The second form of anthropomorphic religion is the Jewish, in which God is at the first regarded as a national God, later more universally, but always *monotheistically,* whereby a new religion could develop from the Jewish, after Greek views had influenced it sufficiently, so that it could rid itself of Jewish limitations.[14]

The third form from this standpoint is the Greek *polytheism.* The Greek religion was at the beginning naturalism (Orpheus); later it became more human (Hesiod) and purely anthropomorphic (Homer), in the idea

12. "Sken."
13. "Praxis."
14. A very expressive word: "Inskränktheter."

47

of a plurality of personal deities, in which the divine unity remained only in Fate. Since, however, this division[15] of God did not, on the one hand, sufficiently curb the human liberty, and, on the other hand, was unsatisfactory to the human consciousness, it was in Greece that philosophy arose.

That which is unsatisfactory in all mythology is theoretical, namely, that according to it the divine being is not qualified to be the principle of everything; that the principle, therefore, does not have its certainty in itself, but in the religious consciousness, which gives certainty to the myth; that the myth lacks inner necessity for the manner of its execution; and that a complete explanation of the world is not found in it, but only answers to particular questions.

From a practical point of view the mythological, just as the anthropomorphic [religion] in general, as to its principle, does not become *purely* practical, but more or less has the character of something individual, i.e. the authority of a certain person. Furthermore, it follows that, even though such a religion endeavors to give sanctity to life in and through certain acts, these, or the religious usage, are restricted to a *few* such, but do not include all of life. These acts can indeed include more than those which belong to the cult proper,[16] but in part it draws it [the usage] into the cult, and ⌐ ˙egards] as moral such acts as do not in themselves include the character just mentioned; but in part the *entire* life is not determined by the *same* sanctity (for example, the public [life] as *more* sanctified or moral than the private). Finally, and

15. Also a vigorous word: "Splittring."

16. From here we have an extremely difficult passage: "Men dels indrager den i kulten och såsom sedliga sådana handlinger, som icke i sig äga sistnämnda karaktär, dels bestämmes ej hela livet med *samma* helgd (t. ex. det offentliga såsom *mera* helgat eller sedligt, än det enskilda)."

in the same measure that reflection develops, in theory and in life, the myths lose their sanctity, and thereby also the practical religiosity, so that human life is separated from the religious, and is determined independently of religion (thus, for example, among the Greeks in the Peloponnesian War, when profane usage took predominance over the religion).

These weaknesses are remedied through philosophy and voluntary morality. Before this happens a change takes place with regard to the myth, in that an attempt is made to develop this itself into something of scientific quality, so that a person, without having relinquished the sensuous, in which the idea is contained potentially, seeks to bring his religious representations into unity under general conceptions, just as *general* practical commandments develop as divine and externally given. By this appearance of reflection in relation to religion mythology comes forth as a science, or dogmatics, which forms the transition to philosophy. In dogmatics the content, or the object, is regarded as given in advance through a divine revelation, and as such it has an authority on which dogmatics bases its doctrines. By this, however, this content, and dogmatics itself, does not receive any inner necessity, but only one that is external, or given from without, by which it differs from philosophy. Dogmatics may indeed wish to prove the myth, and to resolve the contradictions in it. But since it does not in this proceed from the idea or an essential principle, but from the given, which is regarded as *fixed,* and to which one only seeks to give a *formal* principle, nothing becomes satisfactory. Therefore dogmatics leads to[17] skepticism, and this occasions philosophy. At the beginning the latter does not influence the myth, but it can later appear critic-

17. "Upkallar."

ally in relation to it, and then it may have a disintegrating effect on practical life, in so far as it is based on authority.

Then a reaction against philosophy usually comes, because it seems to threaten to destroy the given, without offering anything in its place. Even persecution against philosophy is thereby a consequence of the fact that religion has the form of myth among the masses, because of which content and form fuse, so that a person fears that he will lose the one with the other. Practically, this standpoint permeates all of life, but never succeeds completely, but always leaves withal a profane area, and is restricted to certain acts. The reason for this may be in part the lower standpoint of the given religion, the degree of development of the form, in placing something finite instead of the infinite, since the finite cannot be principle for the whole of life. It may depend on the dogma itself, if it is restricted, since both dogma and the religious practice succumb before science as also before the general morality, as it develops.

At this concrete *development of the understanding*,[18] which as to its content is identical with the power of the imagination, the myth thus becomes theology, and religious practice becomes theological morality. Then, it can easily happen that religion divorces itself from the dogma, and becomes mystic, inasmuch as the first mentioned, since it bases its certainty on religion, makes pretentions at being religion, without in reality being religion, since it is only a formal systematic.[19]

Therefore religion, already toward the end of ancient times, extricated itself from dogmatism[20] and cared little about it, but rather appeared as a striving by the subject to lose himself in God, as a pantheism, but only that of

18. "Förståndsutveckling."
19. "Systematik."
20. "Dogmen."

feeling and intuition; this however in such a way that the subject would not relinquish his existence by it, but would enjoy himself in God without, however, being at any time entirely free from infection by dogmatism. The other extreme, again, is to leave religion, and simply give attention to the dogma (as, for example, in scholasticism), which does not give importance to the religious mind, but in its place substitutes faith in certain dogmas, and the observance of certain practices.

Such a dogmatic point of view will properly collapse before philosophy which, freeing itself from dogmatism by means of skepticism, is an expression of the pure understanding, and attempts to develop an inherent necessary view[21] from the conception itself. For dogmatism is not religion, but a way of representation in relation to it, and not the highest one. And the situation is similar from a practical point of view. Even a religious custom, which is the result of external authority, is an imperfect morality. Therefore it falls in the presence of philosophy, and in practical life, because neither one is satisfied with it.

To begin with, philosophy is low, and it goes through the same stages, or forms, as mythology, but not in the same manner. It supports itself by thought, and seeks knowledge, and for that reason it is not limited[22] to a certain portion of the universe, but makes all objects its own, only that it looks upon them in a way different from that of the other sciences. Likewise it seeks a higher practical principle, which must include all deeds, and for that reason disintegrates, not religion, but its dogmatic morality[23] which is based on external authority.

21. "En i sig nödvandig åsikt."
22. "Limited" seems here to be what Boström had in mind. The Swedish word is "bornerad."
23. "Dogmmoralen."

Here a number of questions arise with regard to the foregoing which need to be answered. What is the relation of philosophy to religion and to mythological dogma, and of morality to the religious cult and the religious usage? and, Does religion in a theoretic sense merge with philosophy, so that this is the perfected religion viewed from a theoretic point of view? No, because religion is the consciousness of man's connection with God and dependence on him in all the various forms of consciousness.

Philosophy is a special expression of a certain capacity, namely, of reason, whereas religion reaches the *whole* of man and determines *all* his activity. By way of analogy, we have the state and the men of science. The purpose of the former stands above that of the latter, and its function is to give unity to all individuals and to the activities in the state. Religion may indeed interpret[24] itself in philosophy, but is not exhausted thereby, but gives direction and determination to science. The same is true with regard to morality. The cult does not simply have as its purpose the harmony of the sensuous in man with the rational, but its mission is to support the consciousness of his relationship to God and subordination under him; wherefore it indeed determines morality, but is not identical with it.

Morality has a special field for itself, because man does not simply have an idea about God and his relationship to him, but also about his own idea and its realization; but this alone would be incomplete and too limited in the same way, as, for instance, if a member of the state, or of an order, might indeed devote himself to his work,[25] but did not subordinate his activity under the state, or take up its idea into himself. As simply scientific, moral,

24. "Explicerar."
25. "Leva i sitt yrke."

and artist,[26] man would not yet be perfected; he rather needs a unity for these types of activity.

An example of such narrow-mindedness in a political sense was *patria* as one only principle among the Romans, for which they might be willing to sacrifice themselves, while at the same time they treated other states immorally. Likewise in the Middle Ages the church and the heathen. Thus, in general, morality always becomes imperfect, if it does not receive its higher awakening from religion, and separates from the merely human what is narrow-minded in it.

Further, how are philosophy, morality, and art, related to the corresponding lower standpoints in each instance? In the first place, so far as philosophy and the myth are concerned, it is to be observed that the latter includes two moments. The one, as principle and purpose, is the religious faith; the other, the mystical form in which this faith has translated itself, is myth in the narrower sense. That the science[27] does not have as its purpose to negate, or destroy, the first moment is clear, because it is exactly the same principle that is active in philosophy, only that this appears in a lower form in the myth, namely, as faith. Philosophy only gives to it greater clarity, whereby it still does not lose the character of faith, but by it faith also moves from something externally communicated to an inner manner of thinking by man himself.

The moment of religion just mentioned—faith—can at a certain stage of development become exclusive; it can become mystical, which is only a certain turning on the stage of faith, consisting in the fact that faith desires to separate itself both from its change of garment which it had as myth[28] and from knowledge, and only desires to

26. "Vetenskaplig, sedlig och konstnär."
27. Boström evidently refers to philosophy.
28. "Från sin omklädning såsom myt."

53

be immediately composed[29] in God, and thereby absorb everything external, without however comprising a scientific pantheism.

If science cannot compel mysticism to interpret itself in knowledge,[30] then it will either descend more or less to dogma, or it will turn into theosophy, i.e. be filled with the content of fantasy. But every genuine thinker is, however, also a mystic, in order that he may gain and give deeper meaning to his research.

On the second of the two moments mentioned in the myth, or the mystical form itself, the science works destructively; and this process is easier, the less the myth has suppressed the person himself and his own individuality; thus, for example, with the Greek myth, in which man had a place and a certain power together with God, but where it also thereby was easier to come to the understanding that the myth did not have correspondence to the idea of God.

As already mentioned,[31] dogmatics constitutes the form of transition from myth to philosophy, as a generalization of the myth. But about this also it is true that philosophy only destroys the imperfect form in which the religious consciousness appears in it.

Such a formal process of development of the religious consciousness as just mentioned occurred among the Greeks; and it likewise affected the Jewish supranaturalism, or the myth, which was increasingly purified, whereby also a higher religion developed from it. In its relation to the Orient the Greek philosophy appears, not only as annulling the myth, by raising the west Asiatic religions to a peculiar form of speculation, Neo-Platonism; it also became a condition for the appearance of the

29. "Omedelbart fatta sig i."
30. "Explicera sig till vetande."
31. Above, p. 49.

54

highest form of religion, even though it also immediately appeared in a mystical form.

This higher religion has the peculiarity that it stands not simply *under* science but is on an equality with[32] it; or stands above the one so far given, and could, therefore, be developed into speculative knowledge. All ancient philosophy was more realistic than Christianity. Even Plato's idealism did not grasp self-consciousness as fully as has been possible, through Christianity, since it apprehended God without limitation, and presented the conception of God as human, by which the development of the idea of the personality became more possible.

But if the myth in its lower form had not preceded, Christianity could with difficulty have arisen. What relation does dogma, or dogmatics, have to science, since such a religion, or Christianity, has arisen? It has no independence with relation to philosophy, because it permeates all sciences, so that a theological science by the side of, or independent of, philosophy could not stand. Philosophy, nevertheless, recognizes theology as an historical-religious science of the given and present forms of religion. It also recognizes that they are few in the community or the race who are qualified to acquire philosophy, or find satisfaction in it.[33]

For the others there is always in theology a more popular form of knowledge, which is accepted in good faith and in the conviction that it has proceeded from God. What was last said is correct, when it has a religious content, with the provision that it always must likewise be determined by philosophy, which eliminates the nonessential in theology, or corrects and purifies theology

32. "Equivalerar."
33. The fact that only a limited few had the capacity for the study of philosophy was a familiar note in Boström. For illustration of a caustic use of this idea see *SB, 3,* 181.

and gives it a scientific content, even if not also a purely scientific form. Theology should not to be able to exist[34] under any other condition.

As far as philosophy is concerned, it is in any case a development in the form of knowledge of the highest religion. Far from destroying religion as to its essence,[35] philosophy itself has the same religion as its living principle; and far from refusing a dogmatic manner of presentation, it rather requires it, namely, for the less educated, but without itself becoming dependent on it, and always purifying the dogma, as well as the cult. Philosophy cannot have the tendency to destroy the cult, but it rather gladly overlooks the less perfect in it, only so that the essential and the substantial appears in it.

The same relation that philosophy has to the myth, morality also has to the religious usage, which rests upon an externally represented authority. Its purpose is not to destroy it, because morality itself has the same principle, but to transfer this principle from the significance of an external restraint to an inner and free willing. Like the science, namely, morality supports itself on the willing itself, or the spirit's own inner law, but in such a way that it has taken up into itself the highest law, without which it would be a lower practice; for it would be either empirical or a subjective and negative philosophical morality, which can arise either because a person apprehends God as a principle of everything incomplete (pantheism), or also if one insists that man's knowledge is limited to the sensuous, in which case morality assumes a limited character.

A correct philosophy does not deprive morality of its religious character, but destroys the manner of presenta-

34. "Bör teologien ej kunna äga bestånd."
35. "Till dennas inre."

tion according to which the law lies outside man, and shows that morality does not have an external purpose. It, furthermore, removes the froth in the practical manner of presentation, which consists in the fact that, either the cult extends beyond its limits, and enters into the practical life, or else in this that morality is confined to a certain sphere of the practical life. Philosophy does away with the view that certain moral deeds are more moral than others. It likewise opposes another frequently appearing one-sidedness depending upon the contrast between the mystical and the dogmatic side in the religious manner of representation, and consisting in this that morality either is used to draw one's self from the world—monastic life—or also in this that a person considers himself religious without really having any true religion, but only by the doing of certain external deeds. But a morality without religion is not a true morality. A common narrowness is this that certain religious people consider certain deeds *par préférence* moral (mercy, for instance), which truly belong to morality, but not as the only thing in it.

The highest form of morality does not only in the first place require, and is not exhausted by the fact, that a person wishes to alleviate the misery or overcome the evil, but that he realizes the good, by which the former follows of itself, even though philosophic systems have existed with this shallowness. Therefore, to accept a holy activity outside of the general morality is a manner of representation which ought to disappear; and a theological ethics beside the philosophical, or free and inner, is just as impossible as theology beside philosophy, and has its source simply in a lower degree of human development,[36] whereas on the highest it is evident that nothing

36. "Utvecklingsgrad."

transcendent exists, but that the supranaturalistic is the rationalistic.

As far as art is concerned, with regard to it also philosophy leads to the same kind of result. Its elevation, namely, consists in the fact that it is freed, and labors for its own sake, or for the sake of the beautiful, without being bound by a dogmatic manner of representation; but it receives this freedom from religion, which also gives it its absolute end, as a revelation of God in a certain direction. Thus religion directs the powers of all men to their freedom, or to the liberation of man from the finite and to the highest blessedness or a reconciliation within man with God and other people.

3. The Relationship to Other Persons and the Race. Evil.

From an empirical standpoint, man's relation to others does not appear to his advantage. Considered empirically and in his sensuous existence, man is a product of nature, just like other beings, and his tendency seems only egoistic, whereby [life] becomes a battle for power and the means of sensuous bliss. [Life] becomes different when he sees his situation rationally, in which case the aforementioned sensuous reveals itself as imperfect and irrational.[1]

Religion requires that all men should be regarded as having come from God, or as having their ground in him or from[2] him. By such a view of man religion already achieves respect for others and love for and attraction to them, and also to God, because God is then thought of

1. "Förvänt."
2. "Ur."

as being present in every person. And clear it is that religion reaches not only to a few, but to all, for "All people are our neighbors and children of the same Father."

The second insight from the religious standpoint is that the same end has been set by God for all people, as for the religious person himself. From this, since the highest end is always present, it follows that the religious person must accept his end and that of others as identical; or is in duty bound to further theirs as well as his own, because the individual end is not furthered for its own sake, but as a moment in the whole. In other words, religion brings with it respect for the right of others, or leads to the idea of justice between people, and of a united direction of all, because no one lives isolated in God, and therefore no one can attain his end except in an organic union with others.

This, as one can all too easily see, does not prevent the fact that the end of one is less inclusive than that of another—as is true in every *relative* system. The one is not for that reason lower than the other, but the difference simply consists in the nature of the activity; from a religious point of view all people are alike.

For this reason, the third effect of religion is that a person discovers that he should subordinate the lower end to the higher and limit it in such a way that in this subordination it performs its duty properly.[3] It is for this reason that the religious person does not experience any humiliation in subordinating himself under a higher; this is what a person actually does in private [life] and in the state. When people act according to instinct it is a common experience that a difference arises between the higher and the lower [order], with the one requirement that there is complete independence for each one within

3. "Riktigt fyller sin plats."

his sphere, especially if the nation is more noble in its inclinations.[4]

When again a person sees that there are not only moral individuals, but also moral personalities, then he also finds by religion that these also come from God and have a divine purpose.[5] He, therefore, has a high regard for them, and is willing to subordinate himself under their more inclusive forms of activity. It is, consequently, religion that also gives man the spirit of unity[6] and this for the reason that his own purpose is achieved to the highest degree only in the community. On the other hand, as soon as the community is disorganized,[7] it simply reveals the fact that man has sunk down to sensuousness, or that there is lack of religion.

Then the demand for empirical equality arises. The demand for equality is religious in so far as it implies that each one is to have a part in the absolute end, but it is irreligious if it implies that all shall only be dots beside one another.[8]

Religion also demands work for all kinds of communities, and thus in the last analysis for the whole human race, but only through and from the standpoint as to where a person himself is placed, immediately in the family, etc. As soon as religion exists[9] in its moments—sci-

4. It seems clear that Boström is here referring to the social orders in Sweden, which he defended. They were: nobility, clergy, burghers, and peasants. These orders were abolished in favor of a bicameral parliament in 1865, the vote becoming effective in 1866, the year that Boström died. See Carl Grimberg, *Sveriges historia,* 3rd ed. (Stockholm: P. A. Norstedt and söners förlag, 1915), 5, 526–36.

5. Boström holds that the state is a rational being—a personality. See *SB, 1,* 378.

6. "Samhällighet."

7. "Desorganiseras."

8. "Punkter jämte varandra." Here we have an indication of Boström's high regard for human personality.

9. "Finnes med sina momenter."

ence, morality, and art—no part is excluded from participation in the purpose of the whole; it is only on a lower standpoint that a person in this respect can limit himself.[10] In this manner religion includes all people as a whole in one single unity, namely, God.

Is the end thereby attained? Is there for man no higher unity between himself and God? Not in our present form of life, because there the race is for him the highest manifold[11] in which he sees the divine unity expressed or revealed, even though he already here stands in relation to higher forms of life, though he is not yet conscious of these. What has just now been said reveals itself in the fact that the phenomenal world is a representation of the essence, and that our earth is merely a moment in a system, and not even the highest in it.[12] Therefore man's effort here for attaining his end is also a moment in his contribution to the development of still higher forms of life.[13]

We now proceed to cast a glance at the relation of religion to the history of the world, or the race as a whole, and its development, where the problem will be the consideration of evil.

In this we shall first briefly indicate the difference between empirical and religious viewpoints in the consideration of world history. If the one who is predominantly inclined to be empirical has attained any higher degree of the development of consciousness, the consideration of nature (which for him is all reality) will compel him to admit that there is order, law, and purpose in it; and since this is a satisfaction of a requirement of reason, he

---

10. "Bornera sig."
11. "Mångfald."
12. A reference to Boström's doctrine of "many worlds."
13. See below, pp. 92–94 and 103–10.

will also pay the most attention to it, or to the observation of nature.

He will, on the other hand, find in the human race only confusion and lack of order, which leaves him dissatisfied, because he sees only the outside; and to such a view history reveals itself only as a Chronos, who devours his children, or as a stream without beginning or end. The past seems to have ceased to have meaning, and the future has not yet received any; and the present seems without being, and appears to be only as an apparition, which already is a nothing, or is in a steady transition toward it; if one stretches out time to infinity, the relation to it also becomes a larger *quantum* of it equal to zero; and if one gives attention to the parts, or to the individuals which exist in these moments of time, they also appear to be without purpose, either snatched away prematurely, or else existing for a little while[14] in strife and struggle.

At times a more calm and more orderly[15] condition may seem to exist, but only for a short while and, as it were, [as] a foreboding of bad weather. On the whole, all power appears as a fluctuation, a struggling, or a moment of eternal change. Even the struggle for knowledge seems to be vain, because the prospect of attaining a goal by it seems uncertain, and its object passes by so rapidly. It seems to be the same way so far as virtue and self-control are concerned. Indeed, if one goes from this reflection upon nature, even this loses the dignity which at first it seemed to possess. It appears essentially as merely matter with certain laws, but without goal, and rather as something monotonous and wearisome.

Over against such a world view there early appears a teleological reflection which lays claim to validity against, or at least along with, the former; and [this re-

14. "Några ögonblick existerande."
15. "Mera lagbundet."

flection] is always a consequence or an expression of man's reason, or its demands, but can be better or worse according to the stage of development of the religious consciousness. From the highest standpoint this reflection becomes the only essential and correct one, and the former [standpoint] receives only the significance of an incorrect form of apprehension. Not to wish to know anything about the lower view is not consistent with the truth; and religious reflection cannot deny the relative correctness [of the lower view], nor hide itself from the fact that there is much in nature that is without purpose and repulsive, just as in the world of men.[16] These imperfections do not make a pleasant impression on the religious person; in fact, it is more unpleasant than the one made on the empirically minded, who only looks to the present, or upon the egotist who is concerned with his own advantage, and is satisfied so long as it can be accomplished to some extent.

But all this can, nevertheless, not disturb the inner calm of the religious person, because he knows that he, the human being, belongs not only to nature and time, but has his nature and his eternal determination in God; and thus he finds a goal and a law for himself, which also belong to the race as a whole, and in regard to which there is no before and after in time but [which are] above it, and are thus sought in all moments. This knowledge in the religious person cannot be disturbed by the purposelessness[17] in the given existence, but [this knowledge] elicits the [deepest] convicion of a reconciliation which the world in itself does not possess.

Thus there arise, first, the conviction and the insight that the human race is just as bounded by law as [is] nature, when we look at its inner being; because the race

16. "Den mänskliga världen."
17. "Ändamålsvidrigheten."

has its ground in God, in whom all is harmony. If this [harmony] does not completely appear in the sensuous world, it is, nevertheless, the essential [part] in it, which always to some extent is present, can be detected, and controls the whole. Thereby the entire race receives the significance of *a unit*,[18] in which the past and the future also are present, and *all* mutually influence each other, even the past. Not until then does the whole become harmonious, even in the activity; and more so in the degree to which reason appears in it.

By this [law] consciousness, too, receives an independent power[19] to exist, and not to become extinct. Furthermore, knowledge and morality do not become vain; because, no matter how little they may contain, they, nevertheless, pass over from the merely sensuous to the absolute as end. The weakness in the empirical viewpoint is that it is concerned with time alone[20] and seeks its end in it, which, however, is not to be found in, but above [time]. This makes an essential difference in reflection.[21] If anyone should assume that the human race simply emerged out of the stream of time, and there also perished, [the race] would certainly be nothing. It is, however, not thus, but this life is only a phenomenon. By this [fact] the whole not only receives a different signification than it otherwise would; but [this is true] even with the imperfect and the evil, to a consideration of which we have now in our thinking come.

Evil is of two kinds: physical evil, and moral evil. The former consists of all such things as are unpleasant for man which do not have their ground in his free will, and of which he, as free, is not the cause. [Physical evil] re-

---

18. *"Ett."*
19. "Självmakt att existera."
20. "Blott håller sig inom tiden."
21. "I bektraktelsen."

duces itself to a disturbance of his [man's] lower nature, without going to his inner being, a disturbance, however, which is sufficiently painful to arouse religious questions.[22] Moral evil again is a work of man himself, reaches to his inner being, or is essentially concerned with him, and is not something more or less foreign to him.

Physical evil is of two kinds: that which is entirely independent of man's will, and that which does not have its ground solely in man's will, but becomes evil only through man's will. The first mentioned is that which arouses pain and which without man's will restricts his sensuous existence, or his rational activity.[23] All such evil is a result of man's limitation in time, which has the consequence that he can only successively approach his goal. This can be general for the race, or again merely for the individual.[24] But both determine each other. The religious person approaches it with resignation, as something which cannot be overcome, either by God, or by man. This is a consequence of the fact that man is man.

Such a viewpoint is possible, if one understands that the world is not a production by God in time, in which case one could always ask why God did not make it better. But God does not immediately produce the sensuous world; it is man that does this, and to demand that it should be better would be to demand that he should not be man, which would be a contradiction. In accordance with this, the religious person is convinced that,

22. There may be something personal in this statement. Boström often, and with reason, complained about his ill health. See Nyblaeus (ed.), *FFS, 4, 5* and passim.

23. There is in this statement a further suggestion as to Boström's own experiences. Though he felt that he should do more writing, and often chafed under his neglect of it, he was so exhausted by the drain of his duties as professor on his limited physical resources that during vacations he was compelled to rest.

24. "Individuellt."

with the higher development of man, the evil will also cease, as a disappearing moment, which will not eternally follow man, and is not an essentiality. Why was I not placed in such a situation that I became more fortunate? This is an unreasonable question, because man's essence is eternal, otherwise it would never have occurred. No one, who understands what it means, would wish to make any exchange with some one else, because that would be absolute annihilation. Since this is true, a person cannot demand that his conditions should become other than they are. But the important thing is the insight that these do not belong to his essence.

The other kind of physical evil—that which relatively depends on man—consists in this, that the natural things and their development do not always harmonize with man's vain desires and plans for his bliss. This may be an evil in a physical sense, but not for the whole man; it is a reproof of his foolishness which, if it prospered, would have a harmful effect on the success of the whole. It is already something irreligious to desire to have advantages which do not harmonize with the whole; and still more so not to be willing to subject one's self to difficulties which are common to the whole.

It is the same with this form of evil as with legal punishment, which, as a matter of fact, is a benefit to the criminal in his struggle against the sensuousness of reason.[25] That, again, incidents occur which counteract noble plans belongs to the former class of evil, to which the religious person is resigned. [He] does not try to do anything but that which for the moment is possible; and he believes that it was not determined that *he* should do *this;* and he knows that, if he could see further, he should find that if that which he purposed, at *that* time[26] and in

25. "Mot sinnligheten av förnuftet."
26. "Tidsmomentet."

this manner, were realized, it would accomplish a lesser good. The sensuous evil is consequently something which cannot be escaped; or it may be proper that it exists.

It is of still greater importance for us that we give an account of the moral evil. This evil could be called sin, but this simply expresses its relation to God, and refers more to the action than to its internal nature. Thus also with folly, although this is more theoretical, whereas evil expresses its relationship to the end of man.

What is moral evil? The following observations will serve to give an account of its meaning. (1) It can never be found in other than personal beings. Nature cannot be morally evil, because the difference between moral good and evil does not, as in the physical, consist of a greater or lesser degree of well-being, but is qualitative, and only exists in conscious beings—even though on a lower level of development physical and moral evil are confused. Evil is (2), as mentioned, not only separated from the good qualitatively, but also quantitatively, which is an important observation. All systems which do not recognize this develop a wrong idea about evil, like the doctrine of emanation and pantheism. If, namely, such were not the case, the difference between good and evil would fall away, and one would say that each, by intensification or by diminution, would pass over into each other. (3) Evil is not as to its essence *one* with the good, and separated from it only as an appearance of the self-same thing,[27] or else it would be another kind of good (thus Spinoza). Neither is it (4) merely or purely negation of the good, as all realistic pantheistic[28] systems have taught, because they have designated everything as modes of God.[29] According to [these] it is only for the relative

27. "Detsamma självt."
28. "Realistiska panteiskiska."
29. "Satt allt såsom modi i Gudomligheten."

manner of presentation, which does not see the whole in its continuity, that there is any difference between good and evil. But [this is][30] wrong, because evil may in this sense be negative, namely, in that it is not the good; but it is likewise a position[31] of something else, i.e. itself.

That good and evil as to their principle are one can only mean that they have not become real for a person, but are considered as to their potentiality; and this unity, or that which is identical in both, is man himself, or his free will as mere capacity; or *in abstracto,* that which, more closely determined, can become the one or the other, but not both. Evil is positive for just this reason, that it is a self-conscious and free activity; but such a one, however, that it is separated from the good.

(5) Innocence is this very condition that has been named, or the will, in so far as it does not yet possess consciousness of the opposite; and one can say that it is a form of existence that man has through God: in himself neither good nor evil, but good *provided* he through [God] is innocence. This word, however, already expresses the conceivability of guilt, which cannot be predicated in God. *Man,* on the other hand, is not good until he has made himself good, and thus has come out of the state of innocence. Because, in order that innocence shall become good, man must make it such, namely by actually excluding the opposite from one's self; otherwise, there would be no action.[32]

Evil is, then, a free will, or such thinking and willing as has a content which is opposed to the good. Such a possibility postulates the fact that man is free before he is evil, and that through his freedom he has determined himself for something that is in conflict with his essence.

30. "Men orätt."
31. "Position."
32. "Annars intet handlande."

68

Evil, therefore, cannot be understood without relation to the good, just as darkness cannot be understood without light, since for both there must be something in common, namely, sight.[33] Thus evil is possible only in and by the good, or thereby that the rational being determines himself to it. Otherwise it would not be imputable. In other words, for its possibility a rational being is required, but one that decides not to be rational;[34] and a free being, but one who decides not to be self-dependent. Evil is thus a contradiction in man, and its ground is the will as a free capacity to determine its being,[35] or not to do it, the consequence of which is that he is determined and determines himself for the sensuous. A being that cannot be good can, therefore, neither be evil; but a finite being, in developing himself, cannot be good without the possibility of being evil.[36]

The necessity of the good is clear in itself, because it is what it is in itself, and cannot be an absolute nothing, even if it does not *actu* appear in man. Evil again is necessary in the sense that evil is a negative moment for the possibility of the good in man—as a condition for the possibility of freedom of choice; and it is just by the use of this, revealing itself in the freedom of the will, that the good can be realized in man.

Evil is, therefore, necessary for man in thought, or as

33. It may here seem as if Boström says that good requires evil; but in the next paragraph he says that it is only a condition for the possibility of freedom of choice.

34. Boström here says that to be good is to be reasonable, or rational. Since God is the absolute reason, to be good would be to be godlike. Since to be evil is to be irrational, it can have no relation to God, and must be the consequence of man's misuse of his power.

35. "Besluta sig för sitt väsen."

36. That this possibility is the result of man's freedom seems evident from Boström's position that freedom consists in the ability to choose between opposing grounds of determination. See *SB, 2, 494.*

to its possibility in idea[37]—although not for God—in such a way that, without consciousness of evil there would not be consciousness of the good, without the good; or, to become genuinely good is not possible without overcoming the evil; in other words, evil has a theoretical necessity when we consider man's development in time. Indeed, without propensity[38] toward [evil] man could not gain the strength of will which is necessary to overcome it.

But from this theoretical necessity of evil as to its ideal possibility there does not follow any practical necessity of its real actuality. That man must know about evil, and have a solicitation[39] to it, does not imply the necessity of determining one's self for it, or of sensuousness. On the contrary, there arises the necessity of recognizing that it must be overcome. In regard to this, it can always be explained from sufficient grounds how it *can* arise, but not how it actually has arisen. In this regard, or as to the factual reality of evil, no other ground can be given than man's free will or its factual decisions.

Thus evil is not without ground, but neither does it have any other ground besides, or any other ground than, the will. In any other case the ground would be transferred to God. Therefore, when we come back to the human will, we have reached the ultimate on this path. Anything else that is found in him as rational belongs to his eternal being.

37. "Till sin ideala möjlighet."

38. "Propension." Boström's use of the word here seems to signify disposition, or will.

39. "Sollicitation." Boström wrote in Swedish and Latin. His reason for using Latinized words occasionally in his Swedish lectures is that in such instances they are more expressive than any Swedish word would be. Among the meanings of this word are "inveigle," "seduce," "provoke," "tempt."

God is said to be related to evil in a permissive way. This is false, because it supposes that God could prevent it, and if he did not [prevent it], then he did not will to do it. But such an assumption is also not needed with regard to God, since we do not accept any creation, but man is just as eternal as God, and what proceeds from him is not caused by God. Evil proceeds only from man's essence, not, namely, in its totality, but from that which is identical in sensuousness and reason, which is the ego;[40] not just from the sensuous, which is not evil, not from reason, which is absolutely good, but from [man] as a unity of both or as possibility to apprehend both in himself. If one should ask why he rather determines or decides himself to the one, or the other, the answer is: because he *does* it. We can perhaps give a reason for the possibility of evil, man's two-fold nature, but not for its actuality.

With regard to the entrance of evil into the sensuous world, it has according to many views been accepted that it had its ground only in sensuousness, in which case it would be only physical; or that it depended on a disproportion between sensuousness and reason, as a consequence of culture and nurture,—but then these would be explained as evil. Leibniz sought the explanation in man's necessary limitation—he could not be like God. But this is to place the will in subservience to reason; it destroys freedom, and simply makes evil a negation.

Kant said that evil is beyond understanding, as grounded in the noumenon, but thereby he merely pushes the problem aside without explanation. Fichte [said that it is] a native inertia in conflict with the non-ego, and therefore a tendency in the ego to permit this to deter-

---

40. "Jaget." Boström defines the ego as that which is identical in sensuousness and reason. "Det identiska mellan sinnlighet och förnuft, nämligen jaget."

mine it. But this is more of an explanation of what evil *is* than of its ground.

In the Orient they sought the explanation in a double absoluteness, an evil *beside* the good; or in this, that the former had fallen away from the latter; but this is no explanation, because *declarandum* is just the ground of the falling away; and if evil is absolute, it does *not* become evil. The same thing lies in Plato's explanation of it, whereby the evil would not in itself be evil, without which it is not explained by Plato whence matter arises. Spinoza taught that evil exists only in imagination. Schelling [taught] that a fall of the ideas had taken place as differentiations in God, whereby evil is transferred to the absolute, and therefore is not evil.

Hegel, finally, [taught] that evil is necessary in the absolute self, and has its ground there, namely, in the necessity of the idea of the good to posit itself[41] or to exist as the result of a process of development, whereby it becomes a unity of contradictions and consequently posits evil, which thereby also itself becomes absolute, and thus practically necessary.

All of these views are therefore unsatisfactory. My explanation—to summarize it—is that man as finite develops himself in time from the lower to the higher, consequently from sensuous to rational. When he thereby has come to consciousness of his essence, he finds two principles or types of forces in himself, which both reveal themselves to him as possible grounds of determination, or are motives for him, although it depends on him which he is to follow.[42] Sensuousness may thereby have taken a certain form, from which it may take effort to free one's self, and one can neglect this; but one can also take up the rational into one's will. One could hereby think that

41. "Att sätta sig själv."
42. "Efter vilken hon vill bestämma sig."

72

there are two forces in man, which war for him, and that the result would depend on which one of them were the stronger. But man is not merely passive and lifeless; and, even though both of these forces work upon him, it is necessary in order that one shall conquer that the person himself shall decide for the one or the other.

All determinism comes from the fact that one has forgotten that a person is not only *a* force, but that, as soon as he becomes conscious of his freedom, [man is] the *highest* power within himself. But it is clear that, if he does not wish to retain his power, then it follows of itself that he is determined by the sensuous or the lower, as the first in time; but this happens simply because he does not use his freedom. We must seek the ground for good and evil *only* in man's will, but only under the condition of the relationship to reason and sensuousness which has just been mentioned.

We add a few observations. (1) Is man evil in himself? No, because his existence in itself is his idea, and so long as this is not his being for himself, this being is his innocence.[43] Is he evil by nature? No, because man becomes morally evil through himself.[44] He first loses his innocence—this lies in its nature—but to it is added a free decision.

(2) The immorality of other people cannot strictly[45] contribute to make him evil. But this can [be said to be true] in the sense that, if through immoral behavior of

43. It is regrettable that some sentences seem confused. "Nej, ty hennes vara i och för sig är hennes idé, och så länge denna ej är hennes vara för henna själv, är detta vara hennes oskuld."

44. Boström's rejection of the doctrine of "original sin" is at variance with the doctrine of the church in which he was brought up. His position is also at variance with the Barthianism of our day. See Barth and Thurnheysen, *Come Holy Spirit,* tr. George Richards, Elmer G. Homrighansen, Karl J. Ernst (New York: Round Table Press, Inc., 1933), 6–12 and passim.

45. "I sträng bemärkelse."

73

others, it can become more difficult for the individual to attain a higher degree of perfection. In that way it is indeed correct. No wickedness can be without influence on others, so that so far as the consequences are concerned, all evil strengthens the power of sensuousness over a person, and hinders him from higher development. *Inherited sin*[46] is just the influence on each one of that which has preceded.

So far as the individual person is concerned, *one* immoral act will not completely estrange him from his essence, but it simply has the effect that, if the principle for the act *continues,* he will find it more difficult to turn about; and this can go so far that a person in this present life feels himself incapable of improvement. By repetition he becomes increasingly a stranger to the essence, and can even find it a hindrance to his present purpose, and develop a hostile attitude toward it, especially during the struggle between the opposing principles, since he knows his true end, but is so enmeshed in the sensuous[47] that he cannot free himself from it. Then, as a wretched person, he may wish himself done with the good principle, or desire to check it. This is one of the highest degrees of evil, although not the highest, which is hardening of the heart,[48] since here there is still the possibility of the victory of the good. The former condition arouses sympathy; the latter, disgust. This, which can happen with *one* person, can also happen with families, races, and periods of time.[49] In such instances a desperate condition arises, but usually there is also just then a turning. He who lives in such a period of time may indeed have a

46. Note that Boström has distinguished original sin and inherited sin. He rejects the former and gives his own interpretation of the latter.
47. "Så inkommen i det sinnliga."
48. "Förstockelse."
49. "Tidevarv."

more difficult time in overcoming evil, and thus it is an inheritance, which co-operates, not for his immorality, but for a lesser correspondence to his idea. Inherited sin is thus not really sin,[50] but only a lack of correspondence to the idea,[51] which implies that one feels the consequences of the manner in which the race has developed. It can, therefore, not be imputed to the individual, but as a member of the whole he must participate in the consequences of the immorality of others.

(3) How is the religious person related to moral evil? (a) he cannot ascribe any part in it to *God*, whether it be under the one form or the other. In God as the absolute good there can be no evil, neither can it issue from him, but only from the being through whom evil becomes possible. Therefore the religious person does not need any théodicée; such a one has appeared only in the systems which have accepted a *creatio libera*, at which the thought has always arisen that God could have made man better, and that with the acceptance of such a *creatio* it is possible to justify God because of the evil in a different way from what Leibniz did.[52]

The case is entirely different with us. Since, according to our view, God did not create man, he can also not have made man wicked. But since man is a self-existing

50. It may be observed that this statement contrasts with many of the pronouncements of the Bible, such as: "Therefore, as through one man sin entered into the world, and death through sin; and so death passed unto all men, for that all sinned" (Romans 5:12). "That which is born of the flesh is flesh" (John 3:6). "Every imagination of the thoughts of his heart was only evil continually" (Genesis 6:5). "For out of the heart come forth evil thoughts" (Matthew 15:14). "Sin which dwelleth in me" (Romans 7:20).

51. There is here a strong resemblance to Hegel. See Hegel, *LPR, 1,* 156–60.

52. Boström holds that God did not create the world, and therefore he is not directly responsible for it. Where there is no responsibility, there is no need for defense of justification. Above, p. 71.

being, he must also in time decide what he is to be,[53] the ground for which cannot be sought in anything else than in himself.

(b) The religious individual thinks of evil not only as his own and that of the race (through the consequences), but as the absolute evil for man, or that which is the greatest evil for him, and in *that* sense as his own. This does not mean that it would in itself be absolute, or that the sensuous life *per se* is evil, but that by choosing it as end man is deprived of that which for him is absolute good. In that sense evil is absolute, and this is true in each moment of time, and throughout all of life, when it is considered as a preparation for the higher life, which is his idea, and the only thing that has eternal worth for him.

Evil is, therefore, for man an eternal evil, because he cannot again enter into this present life and use it again as a means for his end, but has here played out his role, and not used this life for that which he should have attained in it; and also, because he knows that this missing of the mark cannot be remedied by himself, but only by God.

Another question, and a still more important one, is whether evil is eternal in the sense that it must have for man an eternal substantiality or reality. How does the religious person regard evil (4) in relation to *other possible forms of life,* and *in specie* with regard to his own *absolute end?* It cannot be thought that the moral evil will be transferred to succeeding forms of life. Then man would have ceased to be free, and consequently also ceased to be independent, and a man. But he enters into a succeeding life, as into this one, with power of self-determination. But this does not prevent the fact that,

53. "Bestämma sig till vad hon är."

even though he does not need to be *actu* evil, in the event that he has been so here, the consequences of a preceding immoral life will, nevertheless, in part have the effect that in the succeeding one he does not have those moments fully developed which he would need in order to reach a higher degree of life there; and in part that there will be obstructive moments in the determination of the will for the good; that is, he will there have a harder struggle to become good than would be the case if the reverse had been true. This fact, in connection with the consciousness that these deficiencies in correspondence[54] are the consequence of man's own will, is designated as punishment in the popular religions, and, in the contrary situation, rewards.

In some religions there is connected with [this consciousness] the false manner of representation, that outward punishments and rewards should follow. This is a vulgarity that disappears with higher development, so that the punishments and rewards fuse with the consciousness of a self-caused possibility of greater or less morality. Both the punishments and the rewards can be represented by fantasy in various ways, but always with this similarity in all religions, that therein a connection between this and the following life is assumed. In this manner the important influence and significance of the moral evil is usually depicted by means of the most severe pictures of punishment, dim and dark, sensuousness being that which is dim for man. They also picture it as a life of bondage and chains, because the spirit is bound by sensuousness; and this continues in the succeeding life, in so far as it is dependent on the present one.

54. "Oemotsvarigheter." There is similarity here to the use of the term "correspondence" by Emanuel Swedenborg. See his *Heaven and Hell*, Rotch ed. (Philadelphia: J. B. Lippincott Company, 1920), 347 and passim.

77

The connection between the preceding and the succeeding life, and the influence of the former on the latter, finally elicits the question (5) whether the religious person can regard the moral evil as continuing after it has once become actual, or if it will finally be destroyed. On the basis of the religious feeling this question has been variously answered. Certain persons have had a very vague notion about the life after this one, and with these people such a question can, therefore, not arise. Thus, for example, [it is with] Chinese and Egyptians, who accept the immortality of the soul, but sensuously considered. Among the Israelites immortality was also slightly apprehended in a conscious way, but to begin with all reward was limited to sensuous advantages. This manner of representation disappeared in the course of time, but with the effect that there was little questioning about eternal blessedness.

The problem was grasped in a deeper manner in Hindustan, where it was accepted that man passes through many stages of life, and that the present is, as it were, a middle boundary, from which he passes, either to unity with God, or else downward. Then he has a new life-series to pass through, with a sort of circular motion, in that he finally always returns to this life, and *from it* raises himself to something better, in the event that this is to happen. But whether or not this final [state] is to be better is not said. On the other hand, in Persia the express doctrine is found that everything ends by becoming the kingdom of Ormuzd. Among the Greeks there was a wretched view about the next life. The picture is taken from the fantasy that they had about the dead, because the memory of them is poorer than the present existence. They are all represented as shadows, but with a boundary between the better and the worse—and thus, no answer.

Which, now, of the opposing views is the more satisfactory? The thought which is prefigured in the Persian religion must, as the only correct one from a philosophical viewpoint, be accepted as the only one that is consistent with the standpoint of the religious life. If evil should continue forever, it would have to possess an eternal substance, which is impossible. The only thing that is positive[55] in evil is the sensuous will,[56] which rather belongs to the non-sensuous, but only the formal in the same, which also belongs to man's sensuous nature. Since we must believe that man more and more continues in the development of his being, that which does not correspond to his being must in this development be increasingly removed.[57] From *one* point of view, this has been found necessary, but, in order to reconcile it with other statements in the revelation, other hypotheses have been invented, as for example, the one that the evil persons sink deeper and deeper into evil, or into a life of mere appearance,[58] and finally disappear. But this is in conflict with the truth that man has eternal substantiality, and accordingly the immortality of the soul does not hang together with man's morality, but only the *form* of this immortality.

A second reason for the impossibility of the eternal continuation of evil is the fact that many people do not here reach any higher development of their life, so that by far the greater portion of human ideas[59] do not attain any actual existence in our world; others may indeed attain such a one, but give it up again with haste. Yet these [who have not reached a higher development] cannot be excluded from communion with the others; a

55. "Det enda positiva."
56. Here obviously Boström is concerned with *moral*, not natural evil.
57. "Avstrykas."
58. "I ett skenliv."
59. "Människoidéer."

possibility must also be found for them for just as high a development, otherwise this [development] would depend on a certain duration.[60] It is of still greater importance that the religious consciousness would imply a contradiction, if man did not hope that there would be a higher development. The religious individual, therefore, calms himself in [hope of] the earlier participation in eternal life by the one or the other—which would be impossible if a portion of the race were excluded from the development. Indeed the religious person may already in this life find himself living in God, but only as to the principle of his higher life, whereas the consciousness of sin is, nevertheless, always found in him. No one can be said to be so perfect that he can consider himself to be without guilt.

Therefore, if he also knows that he is raised above the immoral persons, he is, nevertheless, not absolutely, but only relatively, separated from the evil ones. But if upon reflection on good and evil one takes into consideration also the next life, this leads to the representation of a final complete difference between good and evil, and thereby also to a raising of the antithesis between good and evil to its greatest height. From this the imagination of the eternal damnation of the evil has arisen—which, however, if it existed, would destroy the blessedness of the religious person.[61]

We sum up what has been said in this manner that, on the one hand, since man cannot think of himself without relation to the others, therefore the consciousness of the absolute unblessedness of some would imply a decrease in his own blessedness. On the other hand, the thought of

60. This does not seem clear, but the words of the text do not afford any other rendition: "Annars skulle denna bero på en tidslängd."

61. A different spirit from the one that suggests the joy of the blessed will be increased by beholding the misery of the damned!

the eternal existence of evil does not harmonize with the thought of God as absolute end of all life. It is possible that certain individuals for a certain period of time do not share in this life, but it cannot be absolutely unattainable for anyone.

Therefore the piously inclined has the conviction that evil may indeed in time work sorrowfully and cause a diminishing of his blessedness, but he also knows that only the true striving can have real success, wherefore he never has more than a relative sympathy with evil, and never any absolute sorrow over it. Neither does he consider evil so gross that it would be a complete lack of correspondence with the idea. To a certain extent this lack of correspondence may consist in a wrong tendency, without being actual sin. Therefore the religious person is careful and charitable in his judgments of others, because the exact state of perversion in a person can be known only by that person himself; and neither does he make too great demands on others.

It is easy to discover that the view of evil, which herewith has been presented, is intimately bound up[62] with the certainty of the immortality of the soul. Therefore, we must also, in our consideration of religion, or the religious man, proceed to a consideration of other forms of life.[63]

4. The Relationship to Other Forms of Life and to Their Totality

In the idea of the human soul there is also contained the thought of a reconciliation and harmony in man between the essence and the phenomenon through his suc-

62. "Sammanhänger."
63. As in other instances, the last sentence is not completed, but leads into the caption of the next section. It is here completed by a reference to what is contained in section 4.

cessive development, both in the entire race, as well as in the individual. When this idea is apprehended by the individual consciousness, it leads to an imperative longing and hope, which is valid for the entire life, especially for the life to come; and the certainty of perfection, when it is referred to the life in time, becomes hope of immortality and of blessedness. Faith in immortality is, therefore, necessarily connected with the religious consciousness, just as is the consciousness of God and man in their relationship to one another. For this reason it has been accepted in all religions, just as it has been taught in all higher systems of philosophy.

It was already foreshadowed in the Pythagoreans, who had the first practical philosophical system in Greece. It is found again in Socrates, and is carried out in Plato. Even if all of his arguments do not seem to be completely satisfactory, this is due essentially only to their popular form. For his system as such, as a consequence of its entire point of view, special evidences would be superfluous. In the popular forms of religion among the Greeks the consciousness of the immortality of the soul was only imperfectly expressed; but it existed, on the other hand, in the mysteries, or the esoteric side of their religion.

This consciousness also has its expression in the Neo-Platonists, as a union of the human being, or the soul, with God, not as annihilation, but as a continuing enjoyment of himself in him. With Leibniz immortality was an axiom, and according to him the soul could be annihilated only by a miracle. It also appears as indubitable in Kant; even though from his theoretical philosophical viewpoint immortality became undemonstrable, nevertheless, as a consequence of its connection with the practical [philosophy], he presents an ethical proof of it, which proof, however, can be reduced to a theoretical one.

There are only two kinds of systems that never can

accept the doctrine of immortality; the materialistic or atomistic, in which no religious person remains, and, further, all pantheistic systems. This is true, in the very first instance, with the strictly pantheistic systems, with which immortality is incompatible, in which man simply has a passing existence in the motion of the absolute, or scarcely can be said to have *any* existence, since it simply belongs to the substance.

But the same thing is true with all such viewpoints as affirm[1] motion in God, even though he is not thereby apprehended in an essentially pantheistic manner. So it was with Heraclitus, Aristotle, Schelling and Hegel, as also with Fichte. For even though, according to these [thinkers], there is something perduring in the motion, namely its forms, this [perduring] is, nevertheless, not anything personal or individual, but the whole could only be considered to be such, although even the personality of this can be questioned.

Our problem in connection with the question of the immortality of the soul does not touch only the eternity of the soul (which pantheism also could affirm); but in addition to this comes the demand that man shall perdure and further develop. The spirit, in relation to its development, is called soul, and as such has within itself an obscure moment. The problem of the immortality of the soul finally includes [the thought] that man is to perdure not only as spirit and soul, but also as person, that is, as an individual being, and thus not simply as to his general nature, but that he shall be the same being, identical with himself, and distinct from all others.

For the rest, it may in passing be remarked that certain adherents of Hegel's system have accepted immortality as consisting of descendents—in which case many would

1. "Jaka."

not have a part in it;[2] or in deeds that perdure—in which case it would also be small or nothing for many; or finally, in the consciousness of the universal human being as eternal, although not perduring in time. Here it is not a question of any one of these types of so-called immortality.

At the consideration of this problem, the correct thing from a strictly systematic point of view[3] would be to pass over from the eternity of the spirit to his perduration and personality. But I shall use the opposite method, going from the lower to the higher; in other words, I begin with the question as to how the consciousness of immortality arose in man. It is immediately grounded in his consciousness of his personality, which also comprises the eternal ground of the expectation in question. At a certain stage of development man arrives at a consciousness of himself as a person. That he is a person means that he knows himself as an independent and conscious being, capable of all his activity, or that he differs from others in a manner that is conscious to himself; this is also his individuality.

In man's idea lies the consciousness about self-consciousness, just as all the other attributes of reason, and therefore also the consciousness of identity throughout all of life, so that he includes in this unity[4] not only the present, but also the future and the immaterial; no matter how much he may change, he still knows himself as the same being. This identity is expressed by "I," and in this he is a timeless and spaceless being. In man's ego is expressed not simply a thought or a condition, but a thought which, moreover, is activity, and the ground of all his other activity, and in that very fact is the [ground

2. Boström remained unmarried all his life.
3. "Strängt systematiskt rätta."
4. "Enhet."

84

of] all that is most certain. It is, therefore, also in this that the consciousness of immortality most immediately is grounded. The consciousness of personality[5] is really[6] the ground of all evidences of the immortality of the soul; they would not have arisen without it. Not a single one of them proves anything in itself, just because they all posit the ego; but they are correct in this[7] that they express various ways for man in which he is able from certain facts to clarify his consciousness of personality, and, with this, the consciousness of his perduration. All other proofs base themselves on certain attributes of the personality, or have their source in such, and consequently lead to the concept of personality, but first *through* this to the one of immortality.

Such a one is found in the fact that man finds himself, as thinking, to be a subject that has determinations, but cannot be a determination, and also to be a being that perdures amid changes, i.e. to be a substance. Now, since accidents[8] arise and perish, but not the substance, therefore the soul cannot, as substance, perish. All this may be correct; but if we recall how I determined the concept substance,[9] then, as a consequence thereof, the concept of personality constitutes ground; and since [the concept of substance] is only an imperfect apprehension of it, consequently the proof suffers from the imperfection that it moves from something secondary, or from result to ground. It is, therefore, valid as throwing light on something that is certain in itself.

The same is true about the argument of immateriality,[10] namely, that a dissolution is impossible without

5. "Personlighetsmedvetande."
6. "I själva verket."
7. "Men hava det riktiga."
8. "Accidentier."
9. "Substansbegreppet." That determination is as consciousness.
10. "Immaterialitetsargumentet."

division, which again cannot be found in a simple [substance].[11] This conclusion also posits the fact that consciousness is one and simple, and it is only in this way that it can prove anything. The simpleness is also a determination in the personality, but only a secondary one; it can, furthermore, be charged that simplicity is only a negative determination, and that such a one is too feeble to establish the immortality of the soul.

Thus also with the other proofs, for example, Plato's, namely, that opposites must pass into each other; if, therefore, death were the last, it would finally be alone in the universe, which is unreasonable. This proves something only if one can establish from man's idea that succession and stages of development simply are product, and that the soul in its essence is eternal; otherwise one would be able to take the same view as Hegel, that life may not cease, but that it is not the same life.

Again, take Plato's proof from man's inner consciousness of the eternal ideas, which he had before and consequently also has after this life—that therefore his being is of the same quality as the idea. But this does not prove that the spirit must pass over into new forms, but he could be thought as returning to *potentia,* just as he has developed himself from it. Plato's most speculative proof is the one which is taken from the spontaneity of the soul or, as he says, self-motion,[12] which as such cannot cease; thus neither can the soul cease to be, because then all life in the universe would cease, which is unreasonable. This is correct, except the concept of motion itself, which posits a higher principle, namely, that motion is not the first in life. But this positive in motion is just life and self-consciousness, i.e. personality.

But even though personality is ground and postulate

11. "Ett enkelt."
12. "Självrörelse." See *Phaedrus,* 245.

of the immortality of the soul, these two concepts are, nevertheless, not identical. The concept of immortality is, namely, the thought of a life perfecting itself in time, and of one in time which is eternal, which does not yet lie in the concept of a spirit, which is timeless. Man must consequently take up time in his eternity. He is as to his essence an idea in God, but, as subject for himself, finite, and thus inconstant, and as such not perfected; and the spirit, as also in itself temporal, and not only eternal, is being and phenomenon, or soul, whose essence and ground the spirit is. As finite, man strives for the actualization of himself, and thereby he receives a nature for himself. The spirit, or personality, must not be thought of as separated from man, but it is his being; or the soul is the spirit himself as active and real in time. Both are the same, in the one case as essence and ground, and in the other as activity and consequence;[13] and it is just with respect to both of these viewpoints together that we speak about "man."

In the consciousness of the soul itself, we now say, is also comprehended the consciousness of immortality, and thus the concept of it; because it is the consciousness of a being that in and by himself lives and works, and who consequently in his essence is eternal. It is for this reason that man's substance cannot share the fate of the merely phenomenal to change; but he is the substance of this change, for which reason his life and development cannot cease. This is the expression of the general thought and feeling, and the problem now is to verify it.

This verification we now gain in this, that man receives consciousness of the perfection of his life in the very fact that he struggles upward to the production of life and self-consciousness in time; but, since this does not fully

13. "Följd."

87

succeed in any moment of time, he must repeat the same act, and thus time is thereby procreated. Since this struggle is intent upon a goal that has not yet been attained, the necessity arises of a continuation of life in order to reach it. This is the necessity of becoming in time that which he is as to his essence, or the struggle of the soul to become spirit. But what he can become through his essence, for that he must have essential inclination, that is, such a one as cannot be separated from him, but belongs to, or is, his essence. As such, it cannot be merely empty possibility, but a force of action[14] which tends to realize itself, or the necessity of realizing all his inclinations.

But in no moment of time does man reach his goal in his present form of life; and this is something that he also feels in that he constantly struggles for something greater than he reaches. Or, the fact that he has an essential necessity means that he finds in his being something more than that which is developed in time, and that he, therefore, cannot be completely satisfied in this, or in any certain life, but only as a whole in all the forms of life which are possible for him. But which time or form of life is for man only partial, and which is complete, is a question which cannot be decided from without, or from the viewpoint of time, but only from the viewpoint of his eternal being; because each time is only a part of *his* time, and every form of life is only a partial one, since time becomes a whole for him just through this, that he actually realizes his essence. Only when this has happened is the being satisfied, and then his time and struggle ceases.

Thus man moves through the struggle to rest and eternity, and this is just the idea of his immortality, or of

14. "Verkningskraft."

immortality in the highest sense, as *one* with his goal.
For, in order to be perfected, man must have taken up
in himself all his tenses; and with the consciousness that
no other [tense] is possible, his life would be eternal, with
the consciousness of the fact that these tenses are successive, even though they are not so for him, since he has
taken them up in his consciousness. As long as we are in
time we must, moreover, change, but at the goal man
should have all the tenses present in his consciousness
as exhausting all the states in which the spirit can move.

Then motion would be at an end, and the content of
his consciousness would be just about like God's. From
this it does not follow that he cannot have the thought of
change, which in itself is not change, but is the thought
of it and as such unchangeable; only as representation
does he have change. This would accordingly be the goal,
and would be his immortality from this viewpoint; but
in his life,[15] or when he conceives of himself[16] in time,
immortality consists in moving toward perfection in all
his moments of time, so that one must distinguish between immortality as a goal and as a *continuous development* of his content. Both mutually imply each other,
although the former is in reality called immortality.

The necessity or tendency just mentioned is not only
a wish which is a guarantee of its satisfaction. Mere wish
is a sensuous desire, which does not lead to execution,
because it is too weak, or the thing seems impossible. But
neither one is true of this desire, which is elemental,[17]
i.e. appears from the certainty of that toward which man
in his temporal development is directed; this is, namely,
to realize his eternal essence, and this goal toward which
he strives is not posited arbitrarily by him, but is of his

15. "I hennes tid."
16. "Tänker sig."
17. "Ursprungligt."

essence. In other words, the consciousness of immortality and the tendency toward perfection are already given in the original notion of man, namely, in God's eternal idea of man.

If we now put together what we have said, it is clear that man's self-consciousness is the eternal ground of his immortality. It is timeless, and were there no question about anything else, no further proofs of the immortality of the soul would be needed. But time enters in, or man is in time, and the question is whether he also as [existing in time] is infinite, or if his existence is just as long as time itself. Yes, because his eternal nature is to attain his essence. This is also expressed in this way that man returns to God from whom he has issued; which is quite correct, because the more man is composed[18] in God, the more perfectly is he composed, and when he has gained this [composure] he has gained what he needs. Then also time does not exist for him, except in the idea.

Before man can arrive at thought he must have lower perceptions, but in reality the goal is that these shall become thoughts, even if they do not become such time-development, which still is finite. But as soon as he has apprehended his idea he has attained his goal; and this he must be able to do, because it is his essence. And this is not something in the future; for God all the stages of development of man are present; but in order to come to the point where he can thus apprehend them, the human spirit must extend itself and its determinations in time. God shall finally become all in all. This is the correct expression for immortality as goal, of which, as perduration, it is the condition.

But it is still not an expression of a truly scientific deduction; for it would be possible in this to think of the

18. "Fattar sig."

whole man as only a moment in a higher spirit, whose striving in him it would be. *This* depends on the manner in which God is comprehended. But before we speak of it, a remark must be made about Kant's proof of the immortality of the soul, which in many ways corresponds with ours. Man, says Kant, feels in himself the unconditional necessity of continuation in moral and blessed perfection. But this requirement postulates that his noumenon is higher than the phenomenon; and, since this perfection is not attained in any certain moment of time, therefore infinite time is required for the advance toward it. It is the same reasoning as we have presented, except that it is taken from man's disposition in general, and not only from a certain one—that toward morality; it is, namely, to permeate all one's sensuousness with intelligence, i.e. to pass over into pure spirituality.

There is also in what we have presented only one other change,[19] namely, that if man's essence should cease, the demand of reason that sensuousness should in certain instances be negated because of what reason dictates would be sheer absurdity, because this demand would then imply that man should sacrifice his whole existence. This again would not be necessary, even with the giving up of sensuousness, when we understand that this life is only a form of transition; then one casts away the lower in order to gain the higher, which essentially is man's whole end. This argument is also completely satisfactory, but posits that man's entire life shall not cease with death.

What has here been advanced are reasonings from experience or from man's point of view, which lead him to belief in immortality. What now remains is to see whether they also find verification from the idea of God. This

19. "En annan vändning."

is possible only if God is pure reason, and man's essence is conditioned, but only *by* him. If now God is thought of as [the] highest reason, not only as unity in multiple, but also as possessing the rest of the ontological and noological[20] attributes of reason, or as to his personal ideas; then man must also consider himself as having the same general nature; that he is conditioned by, or lives in, God, does not prevent this, but on the contrary implies an affirmation of it.

The chief point is simply that God is without all matter and without change; with insight into this there arises in man the consciousness that he can never be without life, or cease, which only belongs to his phenomenal existence. The religious person, furthermore, does not need to understand clearly what we have here said about God, and his relation to him; but he *feels* it, wherefore also it is essentially only the religious person that is convinced of the immortality of the soul, and has need of it.

We now proceed from the idea to which we have come, in order to demonstrate the necessity of several forms of development for man. At this we include the reminder that God must be considered as an infinite reason with the determinations we have indicated about it; and also [the reminder] about man's relationship to God, namely, that man originally and as to his essence is an idea in God, in which he is the subject, so that consequently the idea [God] has of man is himself, as he apprehends his determination in a certain form of his consciousness, but integrates it in his total consciousness. In this idea God can think change, provided the idea is something else than himself; thus his *thought* of change is not inconsistent with the eternity of the idea in him; change can take place in it without being change in him; and at the same

20. See Appendix, par. 62, 64.

time it is true that, in the case that God thinks several forms of development as belonging to the idea, this is not a development in him. Thought *is,* namely, that which is fully developed and as such also unchangeable.

We further call attention to the fact that it is said about the idea of man[21] that it is of eternity begotten of God, or subordinate in conception, but not in time, and that the subordinate is, nevertheless, self-existent, as the begetting—in analogy with father and son. Thus the idea of man is itself also alive in itself, and has its own independent existence, because in God there is only life and self-consciousness. But, since the idea apprehends itself as living and self-conscious, it must find itself changeable, not only in the idea, but must actually experience this change, because it is finite, and by this differs from God; it apprehends its determinations relatively.

It is now asked if in man himself, or from his viewpoint, there can be any ground on which the present form of life can be said not to be the only one. We know God's ideas as such only by knowing ourselves; therefore also it is only through this knowledge about ourselves that we understand that the necessity of change is included in the idea. Such a necessity is given in the essence of man, and already follows from the argumentation to which we have recently called attention. Because, if man were not by God determined to go further, neither would he feel any need of it, but would completely correspond to his end. Just because he does not feel completely satisfied in any moment of his existence, it follows that a higher life than the present belongs to his essence; and, therefore, he must conclude from this necessity that other forms of life are included in God's idea of him than the present, or that this idea is the

21. "Människoidéen."

thought of these in the whole, or of a system of forms of development.

It could be objected that God may have had a higher idea of man than the one of which his present form of life is the expression, but that he has determined him in such a way that he should not ever attain this higher [goal], or his idea. But this is a pure contradiction, because in that case, as soon as he had consciousness of himself, he would also feel that he ought to strive further, but also that he could not attain more than he does, which is opposed to his consciousness of being able to be and become better. Thus we properly conclude from this that man is conscious of his tendency to go forward, and that more is deposited in his idea than he can attain in this life; that in God's idea of him there are many forms of life, not ahead of the present one, but all just as present, although for man they have that appearance.

Immortality is not only something in the future, but as belonging to man's essence eternally present, but by man as sensuous it must be grasped as in the future, so long as he has not attained his highest standpoint. His own determination is successively to become in himself what he is in God, at which the final point would be to have passed through them all, so that all the forms would for him appear present and clear, as they are for God, although indeed, as has been said, this development must continue for him, and thus appear as a before and after. Since the individual cannot attain his goal except in union with the race, immortality and the various forms of life are, nevertheless, valid, as for the former, so also for the entire race, even though we do not know these forms more closely.

The question of man's blessedness is the same one as that of his immortality, only viewed from another side, because both of these needs are essentially one and the

94

same. Man has no need of immortality without blessedness. The most common form of the hope of blessedness is the consciousness that it shall go well with man in consequence of his morality, and vice versa.

But this word can have a meaning of two kinds: either the act of the one requiting, which equates the consequence with the activity; or the consequence that befalls the doer. It is this latter that people expect, and even require or have need of, namely, as the requirement of justice; this is needed, not only as an external necessity, or as something accidental in relation to the deed itself, but as something absolutely necessary, because the moral person is worthy of blessedness, and vice versa. If a person would think of the relationship as being something else, he would come into indissoluble disharmony with himself, and it is for just this reason that he requires it.

This is so certainly given in consciousness, that from this consciousness, or this requirement, Kant sought a proof both of immortality and the existence of God. Although one ought not to do the good except for its own sake, reason recognizes the virtuous person to be *worthy* of [immortality]. Now, since this blessedness is not the virtue itself—it was a mistake in Kant's reasoning, that virtue is rationality, and blessedness again is something empirical—therefore the soul must continue to go on in virtue; God exists in order that he may mete out to the virtuous a blessedness proportionate to his virtue.

This reasoning of Kant's is, however, hardly correct. For it may be asked: Is it true that morality and blessedness are so heterogeneous? And, Is the hope of their harmony, even though grounded in itself, here, however, rightly understood? Finally, Is it true that the meaning of both is the same for the present life and for the future forms? None of these questions is answered satisfactorily by Kant. This much, however, is certain and right in it, that the moral person is not good, and does not strive to be good, in order that he may be rewarded, but because it is the demand of his life to be such; and only such a life as is an expression of this, therefore, has any value for man. But the sensuous advantages, which he would not exchange for morality, do not [have value]. But from this it follows, or is inherent in it, that morality is independent of retribution; and this is even more apparent, if the latter had a sensuous content.

Blessedness is rather only an inevitable consequence of morality and a form of the consciousness that the most moral life is also for man the most blessed. From this it also follows that the concept of blessedness must be changed before it can be endorsed by the religious person, because he cannot wish a blessedness for himself that does not have its ground in religion. Man can indeed in this life feel himself far separated from blessedness, but he also knows that this depends on the fact that he is far separated from moral perfection, and that *in so far as* he has this [perfection], he is blessed and has a foretaste of the highest in it.

By this it is not denied that the religious person may also find himself in such circumstances of life, that he must wish that they were different, such as sickness, etc., and that, therefore, he also can and must wish deliverance from it, and long for a better life. But there is in this, or it implies, a longing for a condition where man is delivered from everything that disturbs his moral life, and can feel his blessedness extended to his whole existence.

The concept of blessedness, consequently, includes two moments. The one is positive—an advance in morality; the other is negative—the absence of pain. This is the concept of blessedness of the thinking person, and that he becomes a participant of it in the measure of his perfection the religious person never doubts, because this blessedness is already present here for man in the measure of his advance in morality, by which he comes closer and closer to God, and is more and more independent of the external. This is his law here and also in succeeding forms of life.

This certainty also gains additional strength by observing the relation of man, in the first place, to nature, as to his own body; for the person who organizes his inner being well, receives greater power over his body and deeper harmony in it, so that the disturbing influences that man receives from his body disappear in the degree that he raises himself to higher perfection; and also [by observing his relation] to the external things, which also are placed in his power, and are made subject to law in the measure that man raises himself. The great revolutions in the earth, which took place before man existed, and the wild forces in the wild life, subside, in part by the deeds of man, but also without this directly, through the arrangements of God.[22]

Furthermore, we think of his relationship to other people. In doing so, we discover wild scenes taking place among savages, but not in the same way among the cultured.

Finally, we have the relationship to God. In the measure that he understands that his goal is unity with [God], the subsequent forms of life also become more harmonious, both inwardly and outwardly, because God is not only creator, but also ruler working with holiness and justice as the guiding principle of man's activity.[23]

This is the ultimate ground of the certainty of blessedness as a consequence of morality, so that in the same measure that man is ennobled, the concept of blessedness is also ennobled, and his certainty of attaining it, but not

22. Like a commentary on Genesis 1–3 and Romans 8:18–25.
23. See Appendix, par. 64.

as compensation for previous sufferings, but as something far higher. "There is a moral hope for immortality, but also an immoral one," says Schelling. The idea of retribution is thus changed by the idea of blessedness into this, that the discord which forces itself into life through immorality is not to continue. It *ought not* to continue, *can,* therefore not continue, since it does not belong to the essence; consequently, retribution consists in this, that the moral person by his morality enters into a higher form of life.

Hereby the question of evil returns: Shall it also continue? A retribution is also found immediately for it in the very disharmony that results from being evil. But its final punishment is its annihilation. It may indeed continue in its effects even in another life, as in the consciousness that, without it,[24] it could have been better; but forever it cannot exist. With the entrance of the good into the world, the evil is expelled, and the evil person is annihilated, that is, as evil, and he can only remain by a return to unity with God.

This is the idea with regard to the final judgment: the evil will be annihilated. This is apparent also with the individual person; at the beginning of his conversion he may feel himself wretched through the consequences of the former life, and the memory of it; but in the measure that he comes to a full harmony with himself, the evil disappears. Furthermore, it is to be observed that even the person, who has been converted later, *may* develop to greater clarity than the one who for a longer period, but less constantly, has worked for his improvement. For that reason we can never imagine a form of life where conversion would be impossible. Such a thought would alone be enough to destroy the whole man, if he took

24. "Annars."

98

account of all the consequences of it. Therefore a final repentance is also acceptance of the opposite, although such a view can be explained simply by an abstract antithesis of blessedness and misery *in genere* and by a representation of the spiritual life without stages, as, for instance, to come to the bosom of Abraham directly from this life.[25]

But for such an imagination, as we have seen, there is neither any philosophical ground, nor any religious [ground]. The latter of these reveals itself factually in this, that, as mentioned, there are religions which have denied it. There are many statements even in the Jewish religion also, which are meaningless without the representation of an advancement even beyond this life.

It could be asked if indeed it would be satisfactory for the religiously inclined person that the lot of the good and the evil finally becomes the same. It does not become the same. Already in the course of this life the religious individual is blessed, and the evil one is miserable—which already is a difference. But the character of the present form of life influences the succeeding one, and this can, therefore, reveal itself there as punishment and reward; and one certainly suffers punishment, even if it is not endless, even as within the state a limited punishment is satisfactory to the sense of justice.

The antithesis, or endless punishment for the wicked, would even lessen the blessedness of the good; it is, furthermore, at variance with the very idea of absolute good. Finally, the race, although extended in time and space, is still only one single being, or a whole, and just as little as the various members of an organic body can be without feeling of the suffering of the others, just as little also the one person in relation to the other.

25. Luke 16:19–31.

One could ask if such a doctrine as this one ought to be presented to the public, and if this would not lead to false hopes, even with regard to continuing in evil.[26] The answer depends upon the purpose of the presentation. If it were a matter of gaining security against the evil, but nothing higher, then it would be proper to use the doctrine of eternal punishment as an instrument of fear. But on the other hand it must be said that it is not necessary to hide the truth even from the uneducated, because in itself it never brings any evil with it.

It is thus possible that the doctrine of the final dissolution of evil could lull some to security, because one can overlook the forms of life that lie between; but the opposite doctrine could also lead to despair.[27] Furthermore, it is not necessary to present everything to the less educated that we do to the educated, for it would be enough to call his attention to the fact that evil, from a moral point of view, is absolutely evil, and brings its own punishment.

Here also we must add some observations. (1) Must we regard fortune or misfortune in this world as reward and punishment, or not? Yes, in general, as a consequence of the fact that the laws of providence put nature in harmony with freedom, and thus also man, and by digression from the right he also brings down upon himself an evil, even if this does not always immediately or in the same measure appear as something external. On the other hand, such fortune and misfortune can seldom in detail be used as a measuring rod for the judgment[28] of goodness and evil, since in part man as a consequence of his

26. Boström's position here is clear and reveals moral courage.

27. By way of illustration, Boström refers to an incident in Dalarna, Sweden, where a mother by flogging had martyred and tortured a nine-year-old daughter to death, in order to save her sinful soul from the devil and hell. *SB, 3,* 280.

28. "För slutande till."

finiteness is subject to many necessary limitations, and in part, further, because the evil and the good live together and both must participate in the consequences of the evil deeds.[29]

The religious individual is in this respect not superstitious either with regard to himself or, even less, with regard to others, because in their case, less than in himself, can he know the relationship between will and external consequences, because much can be evil, which in relationship to the moral character is merely temporary.

In the Orient this view was in force; but the Book of Job has already in a beautiful poem revealed the correctness of the opposite [viewpoint]. The difference between natural and positive rewards and punishments, which are found in man, is, furthermore, not valid with God, because human punishment is also a means of security[30] which God does not need, and therefore punishment has another meaning with God. His will is that every being should follow his elemental laws; then there is bliss, and in the opposite situation misery; both the rewards and the punishments are a consequence of the life itself and thus also of eternal, divine laws.

It could be remarked, in connection with what has now been said, that false steps and folly are usually punished more severely in this life than immorality; and the ques-

---

29. That Boström disavows retribution by God is evident from his statement which is condensed and paraphrased in the following: From God there comes to man, just as to any other finite being, nothing but the good, even though this cannot be realized by him in any other way than gradually, since the finiteness of his being does not permit it to happen at once; wherefore he also must, in each lower stage of development be only relatively good, i.e. also be afflicted with something morally as well as physically evil. This is the only théodicée that is valid and satisfying; because it does not place God in any causal relationship to our human evil, which exists only in and for us and in our sensuous world of phenomena. *SB, 3,* 263–64.

30. "Säkerhetsåtgärd."

tion could arise *as to why*. It is because immorality lies more inside[31] and does not need to disturb the surface, or the end of others; and therefore does not [need to] be so severely punished as external deeds which, even though performed in indiscretion, in a higher measure cause disadvantage to others. Furthermore, it is not to be forgotten that consideration in the relationship to others is a human virtue that is required of man.

(2) Is death necessary for man? The positive doctrine of religion says that it has come into the world through sin, and thus, as it seems, indicates it as something necessary for man so long as he can sin. Death is not unconditionally necessary for man, because it does not follow from his being; from this we also have the conviction in the religious person that he does not really die; but it is only a phenomenal form. But it is relatively necessary as the dissolution of a special form of life; it is an expression of man's finiteness, and by this [also an expression of the fact] that each form for him, as well as for the race, has a center and a periphery. To that extent it is a consequence of man's temporariness, and, in relation to a succeeding life, it is a transition. Therefore the religious person does not long for death, but neither is he afraid of it, because the eternal is continually present with him.[32]

How long must the individual remain dead, since the race and the development of the world are so long? Time exists only for the one who has life and memory, and if

31. "Mera ligger i det inre."
32. What does such a change as death imply according to Boström? It implies that the natural life in man ceases, and nothing else. The human spirit then sinks to potentiality in one of its forms of life, but this can be a condition for the appearance of another and higher life in him. No matter how strange it may seem, one can say that it is nature that ceases to be for the dying, while he himself lives on. Åberg, *BV*, 60.

we cannot say how long man is dead, it is because for him there is no time, since he is not alive; when he no longer continues here in time, then the succeeding life lies on another time-line[33]—just as there is no time during sleep. It is, therefore, correct that between this life and the following there is no difference in time, but that only *in* each form of life man has infinite time *a parte ante et post*.

Must man die several times? According to the foregoing there are without doubt several forms of life, and so long as none of these integrates the full content of man's consciousness, they must have beginning and end. The transmigration of souls has been a symbolizing of it, and one can see in what sense the acceptance of it is correct. It is certain that a past never returns, and that the transitions can become different, although we do not know this difference. But more and more death is conquered by life, and the subject becomes increasingly conscious of the fact that they may indeed follow each other, but that they simply are forms of the same life.

Man dreads death as a consequence of his inner being, which has an eternal force, and, therefore, must find death *in genere* struggling against his nature, although under certain conditions it can reveal itself differently, and merely be united with a sensuous dread. But in general what has been said is true, because each force struggles to continue in its development. There is also a moral and an immoral love of life. The latter is the one that is determined by the consciousness of losing by death everything that has value for the person who lives in the sensuous. From this it is also explained why such a person also easily turns away from life, in case it becomes apparent for him that it is impossible for him to attain his sensuous

33. "Tidslinie."

purpose in it, or if the sensuous itself has turned against him.

(3) Should man be regarded as having lived *before* this life? Man has no consciousness of it, in so far as the meaning of the expression is, if he has lived *here* in this world: if again it is meant whether the soul existed before his life here in time, the answer is that [his soul] did not exist with regard to his present existence, which is a *consequence* of the soul, but that it indeed has existed as to its essence, which is eternal. The representation of pre-existence is an expression of the feeling of eternity;[34] but we do not know this life as having been preceded by any other. If, on the other hand, one wishes to assume that man has lived before in lower forms, it is easy to show why he does not have any consciousness of it. It is because he cannot previously have been conscious of himself, and of time, just for the reason that he stood at a lower point.

Why has not man come earlier into the world? This question can be taken in two meanings. Why not earlier in the race? Because the race forms a system in which each one assumes a certain place. Consequently no answer can be given to the question in this signification, except that his place in time is determined by his *eternal* place in the system. The other question, Why not earlier in the whole? has no meaning, because time does not exist before man.

Why does man discover himself *for the first time* in this form of life, and why does he not know any preceding ones? So long as one *has* the present form, one cannot have the succeeding ones, but one can ask why man does not *know* a preceding one. For one must reveal itself as the first, and the human is the first, where there is self-consciousness—just as man receives consciousness of

34. "Evighetskänslan."

childhood only at a higher age, *ex analogia* with what he sees happening to others without in himself having any consciousness of it.

(4) How long is the later form of life united with the former? That there is a connection is a necessary consequence of the unity of the human ego and of the continuity of everything, or the coherence, in man. But one must not imagine the latter as *simply* a consequence of the preceding, in which case all higher development would be impossible. But a new form is a form in itself, a unity, even though it can recognize a former as preceding; because it is a form in which a new moment of man's eternal idea wishes to develop itself, and it is the more determined by this idea in the measure that it is a higher. Therefore it is vital that man in no life ought to live *only* for the future, just as *"vita"* is a *"continua meditatio vitae,"* not *"mortis"* (Spinoza), because the eternal is present in every form of life.

(5) Furthermore, certain questions appear, which are designed to determine more closely the form and the nature of man's immortality, and it behooves us to see whether they can be answered. (a) Is man in a later form of life to have a body? This is necessary so long as he has not completely filled his measure of time and has all his content under the form of his thought. Thus, so long as he withal is temporal, or so long as man is finite, he has an impenetrable moment, i.e. the body, which always must be an expression of the soul as its principle. But it is also true that he must have "a glorified body," because the more he develops, the more a higher vitality also appears in the body. In order to express or explain this, it has been assumed that there is in man's present body a sidereal principle that is supposed to be indestructible. This is unnecessary, because as man develops to greater consciousness of the rest to which he stands in relation,

he must create for himself a body through which he stands in this relation.

(b) Since man in his very idea is sensuous-rational, can he ever cease to be temporal or in the process of development? In other words, is the progression infinite, or does it finally cease? Man must indeed always consider himself changeable, but it must be carefully observed that the thought about this *is* not the real change, which exists for the senses. Should man have developed all his content, so that further development were neither possible nor necessary, he should indeed think himself as changeable —just as God in his idea of him—but without the fact that this thought were a real transition, in fact, just as little as in God's idea. Since man's content is God, it could here be remarked that this content nevertheless for him must be exhaustless, and thus always a limit exists for him. Yes, he must have such a limit, namely, that something of God's world becomes impenetrable for him; but from this it does not follow that, when man clearly understands what is his true being, he should then need to go further. But, if man has attained this goal, would not the eternal, as eternally one and the same, become monotonous? So truly as this is valid, so long as man needs further development, so little does it have any significance when the need has ceased—just as in God; on the other hand, if man for the present should remain in a lower form of life, this would be unsatisfactory for him, and would bring distaste for it, as all sameness in the sensuous, because this itself constitutes a warfare between the forces which tend toward development.

(c) Will personality continue, so that man will find himself bounded by others as fully individual, or as the same identical subject? Aristotle and Hegel have denied this, and the latter even considered the desire for this immoral. But we deny such a point of view; according to ours, every person is absolutely individual in part through his positive content, and in part through his place in the system, where nothing not individual exists. The antithesis for us people between general and individual is purely relative, or exists for us through the activity of abstraction.[35] But if one turns away from this relationship, every concept is purely individual, since *in rerum natura* there is no more than *one* such. The entire difference that has been mentioned has essential bearing on the sensuous or relative world; within the rational world everything is individual or personal, reflecting the entire universe in itself.

Which powers will man possess in the future life? The same as now, even though in his highest form of life those moments disappear which *only* have regard to time, such as activity, so that the idea of it always must follow him.

(d) Will man remember the present life? At this it may be remarked that man's memory is conditioned by the body, and that therefore with its disappearance, or if it becomes another, memory will also cease, or become another. But memory is also an essential attribute of the spirit, a retention of the former as a possession of the spirit, and the reminder is the ability in the present under the form of thought to retain the past. Consequently he can all too well comprehend this life as a lower form of development, as even empirical examples show, namely, that nothing of the past is entirely gone from consciousness.

I place great emphasis on this, because by this very thing man possibly has his eternal punishment for his transgressions in a previous life, even though he may in a later life develop into what for this is the highest, namely,

---

35. "Abstraktionsverksamhet."

in the consciousness of the fact that the condition would have been better, if he had used the previous life better. If a large surface were illuminated by a light, only a small part of it would be illuminated, if the light were weak; but if it were directed along the surface, all the parts would be successively illuminated, although those lighted up at the first would become dark again as the later ones are lighted up. Thus a part of the surface would, as it were, arise, and a part disappear. Or, if the light should increase as it moves, the former would not to the same degree disappear, as if the light were less, even though it would to some extent grow dim, namely, in the fact that the extent of the illuminated would become increasingly larger. Or, if the light became so complete that the entire surface would be illuminated, then the center would be the brightest, but it would then also be possible to see the periphery.

The analogy:[36] As sensuous, man does not have the power to illuminate a larger expanse, and if he did not have more than the sense, he would know little more than the present; but as memory he has also the ability to know the past, and by means of fantasy to picture the future (without which, for example, all plans would be impossible, which as a consequence we constantly do). Or, if man thinks, he thereby apprehends that which as to its nature is eternal, and which permeates everything that is in time; and the intellect can use fantasy even more completely than the reproductive capacity to grasp the past and picture the future. If man should advance in perfection, he would more and more have the eternal before himself, and the boundary of it would then be that he would move all of *his* world into himself, so that he would have it, not only as fantasy, but as thought. So

36. "Analogice."

long, however, as he exists in a finite way, he has fantasy and sense, and these are not only thought as changeable in their determinations, but the latter actually transcend [the former],[37] wherefore genesis and dissolution are necessary for him. In the final form of life *all* the others will also be present, although this presence would not necessarily be the presence of everything in them since not everything in the former developed into consciousness.

(e) Is there a meeting again? For this there is a valid ground in the fact that humanity comprises a system, in which all the links posit each other. Where? In consciousness. Commonly "in heaven," as that which is not present on earth for the sensuous human being, although heaven is in the consciousness of each one. It is, however, in this not necessary that the same world shall appear to us then as now. It may be the same in essence as the present, but not necessarily the same form, so that we should be able in advance to say how.

In general it is true about these questions that the religiously inclined person does not dismiss them, but rather seeks to find an answer to them, of which he has need. The value in answering them is this, that thus one escapes both dreaming and skepticism. Many have considered it right to leave to themselves[38] the questions advanced, since they cannot be answered in a completely definite way. But the religious person at least seeks to gain a general consciousness with regard to them; and he has such in the higher life which already is present for him, wherefore also the means for finding the answers that are sought is simply to investigate carefully what he strives for *now* as his true and essential good. But these answers always become more indefinite than one could wish. The reason for this is that man can indeed have a sure con-

37. "Övergå."
38. "Lämna därhän."

sciousness as to what has its ground in himself, but that he cannot have a definite consciousness of what for him is not yet temporally present. A general consciousness of the future is possessed by each one, gathered from the present, but anything definite is not possible except by analogy with what has happened to others; thus it is also with the future life.

To this must be added the fact that man in the present life is so occupied with it that he only with difficulty is able to comprehend the purely spiritual in the unity of his consciousness. How incomplete our knowledge of the absolute and the higher really is is revealed by the large portion of the world that is impenetrable for us. Therefore man is occupied altogether too little with the spiritual; the greater portion of the race is far more sensuous than rational, and the first steps in the comprehension of the latter are very weak and childish in connection with the march of development of the whole speculation.

That which is important to emphasize in the present regard is, nevertheless, the fact that the doctrine of immortality has appeared in all religions. This shows that, even though the thought of it has appeared in a sensualized form, it nevertheless is found in the nature of the human spirit, for which reason it, as everything such, has revealed itself as something essential for philosophy. Only in imperfect systems has immortality been denied, that is, in the systems that have attributed relative determinations to God. Another difficulty in the present instance has been due to the imperfect way in which the concept of time has been apprehended, in the fact that one has imagined time as very long, and finally as eternal. Time is, nevertheless, only something relative, which, therefore, in itself does not have any dimension, but receives one only through the quantity of what enters consciousness and is successively apprehended there. This is true about all quantity which depends only on the relationship to measure; if this is decreased, what is measured is still the same.

Time itself does not have any dimension, but this depends on the *quantum* of the content of consciousness and the succession of it; but if a person were able to apprehend all at once, then he could measure the one with the other *within* the whole, but this last would not have any dimension.

We must think of our world as infinite, because the quantity of reality in the world is greater than our capacity, and, therefore, we place ourselves in a certain space of time.[39]

We add a general remark to the previous [ones], namely, this, that the world in time and the temporary perception of it does not *absolutely* perish, just as it does not during sleep; but it remains in and with man, and can, therefore, be brought to consciousness again, which also is necessary, since it belongs to man's nature and development. Further, something [more] is included in this, namely, that in the highest form of life all the preceding ones must be present. The world exists in and by man, not vice versa.

Caution must be practiced in two respects in connection with the questions that have just been considered: the one is not to become a visionary dreamer, and the other not to fall into skepticism.[40] The one who is truly religious does neither one, but stays by what he knows, i.e. the general, and is undisturbed by the other—just

39. "Tidsspatium."
40. The warning about mysticism was, no doubt, also addressed to himself. He has said: "Every genuine thinker is also a mystic in order that he may gain and give deeper meaning to his research." Above, p. 54. On the other hand, he was fearful of every influence where reason might yield to feeling. See Åberg, *BV*, 48.

as the moral person with regard to the future; one is not for that reason indifferent, but occupies one's self with the present. In general the entire temporal life is an activity from within, wherefore the eternal life in man is already present, and the difference with respect to it consists only in the degree of its vividness for consciousness.

With this we have concluded the presentation of man's religion as it is in its verity. It remains for us to consider religion as it appears in time.

CHAPTER IV

RELIGION AS IT APPEARS IN TIME

THIS STUDY includes elements of two kinds.[1] In it we must observe[2] how religion, even though in its idea it is one, nevertheless, partly because of man's limitation, and partly because of his misuse of the free will, appears as several imperfect, or relatively false, religions or religious forms of life even to the point of relative negation of religion; and in the second place we must observe how man is sanctified by religion or continues in religious development, which is the religious life in its existence in time. We can, however, in this part of our presentation only give a brief synopsis of the main points.

1. False and Incomplete Forms of Religion

Religion is universal for man, and is not limited merely to some one specific expression of it.[3] For this reason there arise imperfect forms of religion or religious life as soon as any certain faculty thereby gains the upper hand, or the true relationship between the individual faculties does not exist or prevail. In this regard we need first of all to remind ourselves of the fact that man consists of reason and sensuousness, the former, according to the nature of both, as directing, but the latter, during man's existence in time, as first actual. By an incorrect relationship between these two, such religious forms arise as imply a partial negation of religion.

Atheism may not be very widely spread, but does exist often enough, in speculation and in life. Atheism, if we

---

1. "Innefattar tveggehanda."
2. "Tillse."
3. "Icke inskränkt till allenast någon viss hennes yttring."

think of it not merely in a negative, but in a positive sense, based on motive and principle, consists in a purposeful suppression of the demands of the religious consciousness, and expresses itself either in a certain way of thinking or of acting; it is theoretical or practical empiricism in religion.[4] It always depends finally on the will. Theoretical atheism always arises by accepting sensuousness as the only source of knowledge, and can be caused either by a demand of proofs (in the strict sense of the word) for the existence of God, or by a false study of nature. The one who requires the former does not have God present in his consciousness; and a one-sided occupation with the physical sciences can lead to a similar result; because the more one reflects predominantly on the external, the more life recedes, and matter alone seems to remain. Practically, atheism has its ground in the supremacy of the sensuous demands. It appears in part as *impiety*, a flippant and frivolous treatment of things divine; or as a disregard of them, when it expresses itself in actions that injure the religious consciousness of others; or as defiance and scoffing, when in hostility it turns against God. In part it is *hypocrisy*, when one uses religion as a means for temporal ends—the greatest practical bane.

Indifferentism is not, as atheism, a denial of God, but the recognition of him remains without influence on the thinking and activity of the indifferentist. This standpoint often has its source in early training,[5] since the consciousness was not in time directed to religion; or in desire for pleasure, and in one-sided desire for external activity (for example, political); or if one is brought up in a form of religion which one later considers unsatisfactory, as, for instance, the dogmatic, orthodox, or pietis-

4. "I religiöst hänseende."
5. "I uppfostran."

tic.[6] Not infrequently it passes over into pride or vaunted higher enlightenment than the masses have, and is often more difficult to correct than atheism.

Formalism is not exactly a negation of, or indifference to, religion, but arises when essential importance is placed on something which in itself is not religion, whether it be a certain dogma, or an external mode of action. The formalist desires to have religion, but because the restrictions and not the life in it, have come to his consciousness, he conceives of religion as something which is not religion. This form appears theoretically as *dogmatism,* or *orthodoxy,* which practically has its equivalence in *pietism.* Orthodoxy fixes [the essence of] the religious in a certain *view* about God. It often develops into pride about having the correct view, and often into the desire to force one's conviction on others, and into inhumanity because of fear that it does not stand securely, since it is not based on arguments.

On the other hand, he is a pietist who has religion in his heart, and who protests against locking religion within certain definite dogmas, and rather places it in pious living; in this he has an advantage. It is often united with a truly religious life, but as a rule it sinks down to one-sidedness in that it places altogether too much emphasis on certain religious deeds, which in themselves have no weight, wherewith also vanity often appears and the desire to show one's preference over others. With this the doctrine of man's total depravity through the fall is not seldom united, and his reparation through God's absolute grace. It satisfies man's vanity to be God's pet. Often the view is united with mysticism. One could think that thereby the right view would appear, but often the two simply increase each other's faults.

In *mysticism,* which is the theoretical side of *pietism,*

6. All of these trends have been found in the Church of Sweden.

the rational has the upper hand, but it appears in a one-sided manner, which is also true of two other forms, which we shall mention immediately. Mysticism essentially implies an abstraction from all definitely religious content, with the thought of thus apprehending God purely; but in this one has difficulty in separating one's self from the influence of fantasy, or enthusiasm, which is the same as accepting the creations of imagination as true.

Mysticism is usually employed to designate a religious aberration—that of indifferentism. But even with its faults it is better than the emptiness of empiricism. In a speculative sense mysticism is a longing from the limited to the unlimited, and the drawing back of the subject upon itself; its mistake is that it stops at the beginning of the religious life, at the standpoint of feeling and the immediate intuition. It can be (1) mysticism of feeling[7] and (2) mysticism of fancy.[8] The former stops with inexpressible presentiments,[9] in which it finds the highest bliss and a sharing in the life of God. This is the correct [element], namely, that blessedness is life in God. The latter believes that he has advanced further with regard to a content, but it is an arbitrary [one]; he attempts to philosophize, and thereby vaguely apprehends God as simply a unity.

The reason for these forms is dissatisfaction with the external, and the need for a higher life; the error lies in the desire to come to it in a singular way, and not in the fact that God is in constant relationship with man; hereby the thought easily arises of a select few, or of an inbeaming[10] of God in the soul. [These are] signs of a

7. "Känslomystik."
8. "Fantasimystik."
9. "Aningar."
10. "Instrålande."

faulty activity of the understanding and a tendency toward a life of contemplation turned away from the external cult, and of a disease, because it is contagious. If a person only wishes to follow his own heart he falls easy prey to the power of evil.

Quietism, practically, is the same manner of representation as mysticism, theoretically. It has its source in a vital love of God, but stops at this beginning, whereas man also ought to realize his religion; one believes that one's religious blessedness is disturbed by its being realized in life. But the practical is so essential that without it there is no true religious life.

When people have sought improvement through solitude, it is to this extent negatively correct that in this way they have guarded against external provocations. Quietism has three dangers: that, at an advanced age, when the feeling is less excitable, it easily develops into mere external ceremonies; that sensuous elements easily unite with the religious feeling; that the feeling of humility easily changes over into the feeling of pride. Its general fault is that the duties of life are neglected, which can never be excused.

The peculiarities[11] which are the opposite of mysticism and quietism are to confuse religion with speculation, or else with a legalistic[12] morality. Both can be pursued for their own sake, for the sake of knowledge, and out of regard for duty, and from fear of the necessity of having contempt for one's self;[13] and they are useful for religion, but are not religion. They also suffer from the same defects as, from a lower standpoint, dogmatism and pietism.

Superstition is the activity of religion in man, but

11. "Ensidigheterna."
12. "Lagbunden."
13. "Att behöva missakta sig själv."

117

tainted with so much that is sensuous that religion is falsified. In the strict sense of the word, all Christian religions[14] are not superstitious, but here we are considering superstition only as it appears in Christianity. As such, it appears in the concept of God, which concept can be higher or lower according to higher and lower culture and religiosity.

Thus, God is thought of anthropomorphically when we ascribe to him attributes which are found only in man, and when he is imagined as having feelings and desires, or being able to be led by the influence of man. Thus the usual way of representing prayer, superstitiously understood, essentially belongs to the lower forms of religion, but it can also appear in the higher. The true end of prayer is to lift man to God and to cause him to be subject to [God's] laws.

It is also a superstition that God should be able to perform miracles or change the laws of nature—because in the laws man only sees the commonplace. This belief has its roots in a higher consciousness that is but poorly developed.[15] [A miracle or] work of wonder[16] is an act about which one wonders, that is to say, for which one does not see the cause. From God's viewpoint, and in themselves, miracles are thus unthinkable, and for man they have merely a subjective, and not an objective, significance. The thinker can indeed also marvel, but at the same time he knows that what happens, happens in a natural way.

This is not fatalism, because freedom is also a natural ground; miracles are thus impossible, partly because God

14. Here the word "religion" is apparently used to denote denomination or church body.

15. "Ett föga utvecklat högre medvetande."

16. The literal rendering of the original, "underverk," is used to bring out Boström's play on words.

is eternal and unchangeable, and partly because the laws comprise the common and constant nature in many phenomena; if it is to change, it must consequently change in the whole universe at the same time, because it is the same law in all things that obey it.

Another superstition with regard to man's relationship to God is the faith in a special inner enlightenment, or special revelation, either through the soul's rising to God, or through God's shining into the soul, whereby man should receive knowledge which does not otherwise belong to him. In this there is something that is correct, namely, that religion cannot arise by activity of the understanding, but is always found in the human soul, no matter how dimly. This more vague consciousness can at times break forth more vividly, either by a gathering in upon itself,[17] or by outward circumstances, and is then regarded as extraordinary or supernatural.

The incorrect [element] in this is that man should go outside of himself, depending on the fact that in feeling and fancy he places everything in space. And the incorrect [element] consists in the representation that God does not stand in an eternal and unchangeable relationship to man, and, furthermore, in the external conception of God in space. To the same kind of superstition belongs the acceptance of predestination; it comes from a wrong manner of representation of God as either arbitrarily free, or foreseeing, and implies vanity and love of self.[18]

The idea that God should be arbitrarily free is that he gratuitously determines man, not only for salvation, and

17. "Genom inre samlande på sig själv."
18. It seems apparent that Boström has two things in mind: (1) God is not arbitrary; (2) man has freedom of choice, a doctrine that he vigorously defends (SB, 2, 494, and above, pp. 68–69), but which is denied by the doctrine of predestination.

contrariwise, but also to virtue and vice. Freedom in God is not *arbitrium*. The explanation of God's justice as foreseeing is just as incorrect. History shows, for example, that whole tribes are found on a lower standpoint, with scarcely any possibility of improvement, while others seem to be religious by nature. It is believed that God has foreseen this, and determined accordingly. But God does not foresee in the human sense of the word. If certain tribes are on a lower plane, this has its source partly in themselves and in this, that they previously misused their freedom, and partly in the organic unity of the race. Such a representation of a special election is dangerous, because vanity and national pride easily unite with it in those who consider themselves chosen, the caste spirit in the higher, and dejection in the lower. Those who live in monasteries furnish examples.

A third form of superstition is the belief in good and evil spirits and their influence on man. The reason for it is vague consciousness of God and the relation of the spiritual to the sensuous. There is something correct in this manner of representation, namely, the consciousness that between God and man there must be intermediary beings,[19] but it is incorrect that higher beings, which are beyond man's power of comprehension, should appear and work in his world; no one gets outside of his consciousness.

The view is founded on faith in apparitions, which comes from a vivid fancy in connection with weak understanding, and on faith in evil spirits; it has its cause partly in this, that he is unable to explain evil from the physical reasons for it, and partly in the fact that he is led to bad deeds by his own desires, and later, when reflexion sets in, he finds that he did not wish to do so,

19. "Mellanvarelser."

and then tries to remove the blame from himself; finally [the view is founded] on this, that an evil spirit should have deceived man, who was by God created perfect, to become evil; but man is neither created by God, nor is he, except in his idea, perfect. Even though the belief just mentioned has been widespread, it only proves that the cause has been widespread.

Another superstitious view is the one about angels, a sensualizing of the omnipresence of God; the sensuous in this is to think either that God is not powerful enough or that he is too exalted to do everything. The imagination about guardian spirits is a sensualizing of man's own higher nature. The belief that the pious departed should effect with God through prayers what man himself cannot do is superstition; man as sensuous thinks himself as standing nearer to the lower beings than to God, and that it is, therefore, easier to turn to them than to God himself.

A further form of superstition is this, that man clothes the spiritual in a material form, usually that which he here regards as the highest good or evil. Thus, for example, the imagination about Hades, Purgatory, an interim between death and the judgment, etc.

Some think of the world as a vale of woe[20] and heaven as a hall of bliss,[21] which shows that they do not here find their rational needs realized, but also that they have not grasped the significance of this life. According to Christianity, God's kingdom comes to us, not we to it. There are, furthermore, many other forms of superstitious imagination, for example, that blessedness consists of something different from the religious life, or that man as a consequence of immorality can suffer something worse

20. "Jämmerdal."
21. "Fröjdesal."

than the diminution of spiritual life; all of which has its ground in the preponderance of the sensuous over reason.

2. *The Effect of Religion on Man and the Means for It*

Religion, in so far as it is real in man, is activity. God is not in himself active, but rather in relation to man, i.e. in man's relation to him, which indeed is consistent with God's immutability. Religion is an activity to determine the lower according to the higher. Action is either by man or by God; here the two fall together. All activity moves from a principle to a goal; here reason, or God, is both. The activity of religion consists in realizing one's self in the sensuous, or to change this in such a way that it becomes an organ or a form for the activity of reason; just as the activity of the individual in the community, by working in agreement with it, becomes public.

There are various names for this. One is *redemption,* which is based on the Oriental representation of war between the good and the evil, as well as the fact that man at some time should have been perfectly good. Another is *deliverance,* which implies that man is bound by the sensuous, and that only reason gives him independence; *salvation*—that the sensuous life is an evil; *conversion*—that man must change the point of direction[1] in his activity; *justification* and *sanctification* (by partaking in the holiness of God): with regard to the consequences.

The ultimate ground for the effect of religion on man is not man's temporal, but his eternal, nature in God, and can be considered as to its essence and its expressions in the individual and in the race. This ground is called

1. "Riktningspunkt."

in theology *vocatio,* which man does not have as sensuous, but through his essence in God, i.e. from God; from this *vocatio secundaria* must be differentiated, which is based on the former, and occurs in certain moments of time. This is *vocatio generalis,* extended to all through the Christian doctrine; however, beyond this doctrine, [the call] also advances to the heathen, although less clear and active (this against the Calvinists).

It [the *vocatio*] must finally reach its goal, even if not in this form of life. These works are in theology called God's works of grace, which is correct, even though the expression can lead to the misapprehension that it is an act of God which man without him would not be able to achieve, which is grace in the theological sense; but all *arbitrium* on the part of God must be strictly separated from it [grace].

As a consequence of this general call every person must be certain of his salvation; God cannot fall short of his goal, i.e. evil is not fundamental. With such a doctrine the doctrine of the final judgment in a strict sense is at variance; but it is not certain that this doctrine comes from Christ himself, but from the authors of the Gospels; it is also only a parable about the relationship between the evil and the good.

Furthermore, it is observed here that with this doctrine there would be need of a special order of grace also in the next world—but the scriptures do not speak of such a one. For us, from the standpoint just given, there is no need of anything such [as grace]. Such an order of grace would not be needed because even the best are not worthy and mighty to enter the highest blessedness. One could say that God could forgive them, but this is based on the false view that salvation is conceivable without man's free cooperation, or consists in something else than actual religion.

It could be observed that this doctrine just proposed by me about the unconditional salvation of all is dangerous because it induces a sense of security; but this can only be true in the case of the one who already is evil, and thus would be led to continue in his evil. But it is never worth while to keep silent about the truth to save anyone; and through fear no moral, much less spiritual, improvement is ever made. Evil, without being eternal unblessedness, can, nevertheless, be as great as sin; it is, furthermore, well known that the better a person is, and the more insight he has into the spiritual life, the deeper repentance does he feel for that which has been neglected.

It could further be observed that the doctrine often mentioned[2] is at variance with the morally strict spirit of Christianity, which definitely separates between good and evil, since here, on the other hand, all would come out the same.[3] To this it is already replied: It is not the same if I am fully well, or only after sickness can gain my health. Each one has to suffer what he deserves, and only through repentance is salvation attained; thus the good and the evil are absolutely separated.

It can also be remarked that the doctrine would minimize the call of God. No, but the exclusion of one single person would minimize the blessedness of the blessed— as Schleiermacher properly remarks. God is never absent from any human being, which is an idea that only bases itself on the empirical thought that God, after he had created man, left him to himself; but without his idea man would be absolutely nothing. The human race is one single organic whole, where the one part cannot be separated from the other, but whatever anyone has done

---

2. "Meranämnda."
3. "Komma ut på ett."

of good or evil, he has done it for the whole race, and the very misery of the evil is a benefaction, and drives to repentance.

Repentance is the condition for redemption, and means the acceptance of a new principle for one's life, which is repentance in the narrow sense; in the wider [sense] it is the advance of the entire person to a higher [life]. The question has been raised as to whether a man can convert himself; this was the concern of the strife between Pelagius and Augustine. That he can is proven by the fact that he has consciousness of the command to do so; as free he can also tear himself loose from the sensuous and decide on the one thing,[4] and if he does not do this in the present life, being sunken in sensuousness, then in another form of life. Conscience[5] is both a summons to repentance and a witness to its possibility, wherefore also man always has the consciousness of good and evil; otherwise he would be absolutely annihilated, which is impossible, since he is of the essence of God.

The doctrine of man's incapacity with regard to repentance depends upon an abstract conception of God and his relationship to man, namely that of thinking of the sensuous as man's nature and of reason and God as outside of him. This view does not find any support in the doctrine of man's corruption; if he were absolutely corrupt, he would not feel the need of repentance, but the expression of sorrow for the corruption shows that it has not gotten hold of the whole man. Many have zealously defended this doctrine, which is a repulsive expression of self-love, as if one would place more value on what has been received through grace than by one's

4. "Ettdera."
5. Regarding conscience Boström says that it does not decide between right and wrong, but is concerned only with the pleasant or unpleasant. *FE,* 91.

own labors. Thus it happens in relation to despots. Analogous with this is the excess with which the converted speak of their wickedness before conversion.

But, irrespective of the fact that man has the power of conversion, a conversion without God is inconceivable. In this lay the common mistake of Pelagius and Augustine, namely, to place man outside of God, and then ask what he could do, which is an absurdity.[6] Pelagius consequently placed salvation in something else than the religious life, which is heathenish. If by man's own power a power were meant that is not also God's, then it would not be good, and man could not by it be converted.

The sensuous man does not reform himself, but is reformed by the higher nature that is in him; and it is not conceivable that two beings can work together toward one goal; this is shown by the community and the citizen. Without taking God into himself, man cannot become religious, but it is also God who is present in man and causes conversion; this is not something that has come from the outside, but develops from within and has of eternity *potentia* existed in man. The two statements are united in this, that man is converted by God, who is in him, and that man acts quite humanly.

As far as conversion, as it appears in time, is concerned, it is given and complete in his [man's] inner being as soon as he has made God the principle of his life. But he can also be considered from the viewpoint of the multiple with regard to his life as a whole. According to the first viewpoint, each act has its own consequences, and conversion is *one* act; but, viewed from the viewpoint

6. Boström here reveals a valuable insight. Salvation cannot be divorced from the religious life. One is reminded of Paul's words: "Work out your own salvation with fear and trembling; for it is God who worketh in you both to will and to work, for his good pleasure." Philippians 2:12–13.

just mentioned, the conversion is grounded in a multiple of decisions and is carried out in a multiple of acts.

After man has determined to reform, he has peace, but this decision does not occur all at once, but gradually, and even thereafter he, therefore, has a struggle and battle, and a relapse is possible. For that reason man also needs external means of help, which by the providence of God, or God's presence and successive development in the world, are not wanting; thus [we find it] in the church, the family, the state, the union of states, and world history. These are the summing up of God's external workings of grace, and the one who does not neglect[7] them receives unmistakable efficacy from them.

Many people are not essentially evil or indifferent to religion, but still sensuous egoists; in them a conversion is not really necessary, but only a continuous development of the higher life, by suppression of the sensuous, which, however, is always accompanied with some suffering. Others slave under sensuous passions, which must be uprooted through strife and struggle, in which one is not always the victor, nor achieves it without noticeable consequences.[8] For this reason it has been said that man must experience contrition before he can repent.[9] Evil always brings its own punishment, if not here, then in another form of life, where the good appears more clearly.

Reconciliation is repentance, because the consciousness of God brings disharmony to the sensuous person. Since salvation is a work of God, one must from this side say that he reconciles man through his eternal love, as principle for [man's] higher life. Reconciliation results in deliverance from sin, and thereby from its punish-

7. "Ej lämnar dem å sido."
8. "Kännbara följder."
9. "Kan bättras."

ment, and not only [from] the latter [i.e. punishment]. The servants of the church can consequently never grant the forgiveness of sins, or reconciliation, to the one who does not himself have the power of repentance.

The workings which have now been mentioned are the same for all people, and for the entire race, for which reason all people have had a consciousness of the need of repentance, and have regarded it as of the greatest importance. It is necessary for all; all must take part in the doing of penance, i.e. in suffering and disharmony because of sin. The best person will consequently suffer the most for the sin of all; but this is not a positive evil, for he will afterward enter into so much the greater glory; and it works so much the more for the improvement and sanctification of all.

The next question will concern the means which man employs for the attainment of the religious goal. False ones are, for example, reconciliation through discipline. The reason for prescribing them is the thought that man for repentance needs to keep his sensuous nature under discipline, to which is added [the fact] that he feels the need of reconciliation through chastisement as causing sorrow and pain. The false element in it is to consider the chastisement necessary and good in itself; therefore contrition is also considered sufficient among the more cultured. The contrary view depends on the fact that God is regarded as a despot. In the more sensuous person, who imagines that the evil comes from without, this conviction leads to faith in the necessity of physical chastisement of himself, partly to place himself in opposition to the external world, and partly in order to set himself against his own sensuous nature.

But it is foolish to deprive one's self of the means of help, in order to set one's self in opposition to the sphere in which religion is to be realized, and injurious to true religion, because in this way man makes himself more and more incapable of it. It can, furthermore, easily happen that [man's] nature treated in such a hostile manner turns inimically against man, which can proceed even to madness, just as in general it is natural that the sensuous powers, if they are not employed as means for the rational, will take another turn. The only helpful external measure is activity, wherefore also hermits, and such, have complained the most about temptations, whereas the active person does not have time to feel[10] them. To this further belongs the belief that matter is the principle of evil and the organ by which evil spirits tempt man. Such a belief easily passes over into vanity and to faith in some merit, and a desire of admiration by the multitude. True ennoblement never has this result,[11] because it is never absolute and never occurs without the help of God.

Religion does not require of man any sorrowful moments[12] for their own sake; the one who has attained the religious life can move about in the external world with security and joy. The doing of penance is often a necessary consequence of conversion, but is not in itself a principle or a necessary condition. Another measure that is often urged is sacrifice—gifts brought to God in order to win a friendly relationship with him; or love and gratitude in order to win his grace; or as reconciliation for transgressions.

The first mentioned may take place even in the higher religions, but only with a symbolic signification; the last named comes from the concept of him as despot. It arises through the belief that we must make amends for sin, in which the false [idea] is this, that this could come

10. "Känna efter dem."
11. "Leder aldrig dit."
12. "Sorgsna stunder."

through anything else than repentance. In gloomy forms of religion there are in this respect not only personal sacrifices, but also the acceptance of substitutions, which are supposed to be more effective and better, the more costly they are: from which we have human sacrifice.

This form of representation is united with a certain activity of the fantasy; sin rests heavily on man, and he as it were, suffers with the one sacrificed, who by his lesser guilt would have the right to claim some kind of merit. In addition, [this form of representation] is united with the idea of the connection between the blood and the life, and that by draining the warm blood one should rather mean the life.

Finally, there is also connected herewith the idea that God indeed is loving, but also just,[13] and that one arouses sympathy in him by punishing one's self; and also that he is offended, and therefore less kindly disposed toward man. But God's justice is one with his love.

It is now asked if sacrifice has any side from which it ought to be retained. It may have the symbolical meaning that we have all from God, and that all ought to be subjected under him. But the only real sacrifice is [the giving up of] sensuousness, provided it is in disharmony with reason, although this can only by mistake be considered as equivalent to repentance. By such a sacrifice man does not lose his sensuousness, but it is only this, that sensuousness should not be the end, or something essential, but that he rather gains by the sacrifice of the sensuous.[14] Occasionally religion may even require the sacrifice of the entire sensuous life, but this life is from a religious point of view of no essential significance, and thereby

13. Doctrines of the Church of Sweden.
14. "Människan förlorar med ett sådant offer ej sin sinnlighet, utan endast det, att sinnligheten skulle vara ändamål, eller något väsentligt, vilket hon tvärtom just genom offrandet av det sinnliga vinner."

man attains just that for which the sensuous life exists, and it would be foolish to sacrifice the end for the means. From what has been said the importance of the doctrine of immortality can be seen, [a doctrine] which is so important for man's morality that, if it did not exist, the whole man, as Plato says, would be a contradiction.

All the acts belonging to the religious cult, such as prayer and the church, are, furthermore, means for the influence of religion upon man. The church is a house where people gather for divine service. Further, in a transferred[15] sense, [it is] a moral personality, the congregation extended into the signification of the unity of the people, who confess the same religious teaching. [The church], finally, receives a still wider significance, that of all people; as such, it has its unity from within, including all people in whom religion exists and is active, in the last analysis, in all humanity.

Here we think of the church appearing in the sensuous world, a community of people, among whom the same religion prevails. The church, in this sense, is thus (1) unity of rational beings, (2) a rational community, which has reason as ground, law, and end, and consequently the same attributes as reason. It is, therefore, not an association, but a community. There are two kinds of these: private and public. The church is not any special one of these; it is the unity in all, i.e. all are communities only to the extent that they comprise more limited forms of the highest community, the church. Each community is, therefore, a church, provided it assumes the highest human end, religion, which does not exclude the possibility that it likewise is a special [religion]. If this is true, one may ask wherein the difference between church and state exists. It has an historical ground. In ancient times

15. "Translat."

people did not know any difference between them. But at the spread of Christianity the state was heathen at the beginning, and from this came the idea that the church was something higher and more noble than the state, which was only worldly. In the Middle Ages the battle was essentially not between church and state, but between the private communities which wished to maintain their right *against* the state, and the state or the public; thus also with the order of the priesthood, whose members were the functionaries of the church, but who had usurped the right of the church, and who themselves wished to be regarded as having this right, or comprising it. Protestantism united church with state, which is church in an eminent sense, because it is an independent community, which does not need to be integrated by others. Every state is essentially a church, and if *one* is spread over several states, this means only that it is common to all.

Every church has a definite doctrine, or confession, i.e. a definite theoretical manner of representation of God. Every religion also necessarily has a cult, i.e. a unity of acts, which are directly designed to lift man to God, and with respect to his will to subject it to God's. Cult and doctrine cannot be separated, because they mutually determine each other, although the one, especially in the lower forms of religion, can be preponderant, as for example, the cult among the Greeks. Neither one is anything accidental, even though certain moments in it may seem to depend on *arbitrium*. The church should never forget that it is a living being, which is to be developed in time. For that reason there must be no norms, which prevent such a development, because then they are deserted by people, and it causes divisions, since they no longer find themselves fully satisfied in it. Confession should, therefore, touch only the general, which is given for a certain time in the religious consciousness, as a symbol or norm of doctrine for the priests. Certain attributes of reason[16] should be required of the ministers to prevent error, but not in such detail that there is no freedom for feeling and imagination. An order of clergy is necessary, since there is in religion a unity of the theoretical, practical, and esthetic, which is represented by the ministers.

The question is now raised as to what means the church has for the attainment of its goal. The Word and the Sacraments. Both ought to be purposeful for a definite time. Further, living organisms, the servants of the church, [who are] "spiritual," since they work especially for the purpose of the church. Their responsibility is to keep the doctrine and the cult in power, and to communicate it to the congregation.

The teachers must necessarily comprise a separate order. The regent is at the head of it, but not himself a teacher, because the general is only determining for the individual. The state does not in fact have ministers, except the highest, who have general guidance of all that belongs to the church.[17] The rest have their place in the community, and even larger families may wish to choose organs for their religious activity, namely, home preachers.[18] The highest functionaries of the church itself participate less in the execution of the divine service than in the guidance of the whole of it. Under these we have the entire spiritual order, thus also men of science, artists, and others.

A distinction must, however, be made between the last named and those who work directly for the arousing of the spiritual consciousness and for the care of souls. The religious activity is a unity of theory and practice, and

16. "Förståndsbestämningar."
17. "Det kyrkliga hela."
18. "Huspredikanter."

therefore the servants of the church should also have scientific training. Herein is revealed the difference between men of science as such and teachers of religion. There should be no secrets, but everything should be revealed to the people; the ministers are not definitely separated from the others, not holier, as if they were nearer to God; therefore they must not build a hierarchy.

The spiritual order is political, provided it carries out deeds enjoined by the government;[19] in other respects it is a private order. From this it comes that, as a rule, the ministers are appointed by a choice of the congregation, although, since it is not certain that thereby in all cases the right is done, there is reason why the government has reserved the right of appointment in some cases.[20]

The ministers should not fall into any kind of formalism, i.e. consider the teaching and the worship as something holy in itself, but rather the spirit as leading to blessedness. The opposite fosters a caste system.[21] They must be careful not to impart superstitious ideas, as, for instance, that the sacraments have any miraculous power; they should not work exclusively on the feeling; nor should they teach philosophy, although clarity in the teaching is most highly important to strive for. Extremes in this regard are formalism and mysticism.

Founders of religion or reformers are such men as especially express the religious consciousness of their age; such men have been found in all ages, but those who have been epochal have naturally had an influence on man's entire life, since religion is its principle. That the old forms should rise in opposition at the appearance of a reformer is natural, especially since reformers appear

19. The minister in Sweden, for instance, issues certain certificates that are here issued by the state.
20. For instance, the archbishop is appointed by the King.
21. "Kastväsen."

at times of great religious abuses, and when the time is far advanced without a like advance in the forms of culture. The reformers have their authority from within, from God, and do not need any external authority.

What right and power does the church have in general, and what external means should it employ for the furtherance of its end? The same as the state itself, and it can thus also defend itself with force against attacks against its objective laws. These general laws bear upon jurisprudence, whereas, with the question of conviction as to the religiously and morally right, the right of force falls, since it is impossible, because the essential is free and independent. But an irreligious act can indeed be such that one can understand that, if it were permitted to continue, it would be inconsistent with the very continuance of the state, and then forceful means are necessary, not for the sake of improving the criminal, but in order to stay the consequences.[22]

The right of the state with regard to confession is that the church must have certain norms for its confession. Therefore it is properly punishable[23] if anyone falls away, or spreads contrary doctrines, or sets a poor example. Deviations, however, can be tolerated so long as they do not touch anything essential. The punishment here is naturally exile. But this is not really punishment of the individual, whose faults are based on theoretical conviction, but is established for the security of the state. If the one who has fallen away changes his convictions, the punishment is cancelled.

In what has been said it is not a contradiction that other confessions are permitted within the state, which,

---

22. From this point of view. Elsewhere Boström has said that the purpose of punishment is the improvement of the offender. *SB, 3,* 266–75, especially 272.

23. "Belagt med straff."

in the measure that the state is sound, can be tolerated, however, without the right of their members to manage the offices of the church or the state, and with the provision that they do not strive to make proselytes, and with such a purpose turn to the non-thinking. But when one who falls away thereby gives a poor example to those who are uncultured and indifferent, he places himself in the same relation to the state as a person who is not a citizen; wherefore the state must investigate whether he should be permitted to remain in it, which should not be permitted, if he can be proved to be eager to make proselytes. The right of the church in this does not, however, extend beyond the right of the state, because [the right] of no one goes beyond it. No one can, therefore, be said to have fallen away who has not declared it. The church has the right to maintain a certain discipline, and for that reason it can deny certain advantages to the one who has revealed himself as not possessing a religious attitude. The church certainly has the same right as other communities to protect itself against others, but only the state can decide about the right to use force and the general conditions for it.

A holy catholic church is to this extent a correct representation, if one means thereby that the various churches simply are manifestations of only one; or as it is the expression of faith in the possibility and actuality of religion in the race in general; or in the appearance of that which is eternal in a church bringing salvation to man. Religion saves, and the church is religion in its complexity, i.e. it appears in many persons who have the same conviction; and in this sense, consequently, the church saves. But, on the other hand, [to say] one certain church should be the only one that has salvation is a mockery against Providence, and this so much the more, as this church can claim age,[24] whereas humanity constantly moves forward.

It remains to speak about *the divine revelation*. Revelation reveals that which is not hidden, but which is, or can become, familiar, which is known, or can be known. All knowledge is thus revelation, and revelation is, consequently, either an activity in the one who reveals, or a quality in that which can become known, or both, and their cooperation.

Divine revelation, then, becomes the act through which God becomes known, or at least possible of being known; [it is] that quality in God through which it is possible to know [him]; or [it is] God's being, provided it is possible for man to learn to know [him], and the comprehension of man's knowledge of him. Such a [knowledge] must exist in the world, provided there are rational beings; man does not know God because he is rational, but he is rational because God's essence is present in him (because nothing exists *outside* God); he must, therefore, always be more or less clear to man; and by man's reason is meant just his complete perceptions.

God is revealed to man through himself in this way, that he is in man, and man in him; that is to say, man comprehends himself in relation to God, i.e. comprehends him. This relationship is eternal. In time it reveals itself as man's development toward rationality, and is, therefore, successive. By that which is divine in man God consequently reveals himself to him. At times it has not been possible to understand this, because man has been placed in one space, and God in another, and then a revelation *extra ordinem* has been required. Originally, revelation is from God's side, even though successive on

24. "Har åldern för sig."

man's. God has also originally revealed himself in a perfect way, or, in his revelation eternally reached his goal, and a higher revelation than the one through God is impossible. From man's side again this revelation must be successively realized, through interaction with external nature; this must be done, however, with the provision that in this he also lives in interaction with other people; and this successive revelation is history, seen from the highest viewpoint.

A special divine revelation must mean, either such a one as would be separated from the original relationship between God and man, and given for some special purpose; or one that had its ground, not in this relationship, but in some immediate contact between God and man in a certain time, and which only had validity for it. As reason for such a one could possibly be alleged man's need of it, and this can appear to be a correct point of view. One has thereby said that God's original revelation was not sufficient. On the other hand, this shows itself at war with the fundamental principle of religion. Creation must then be regarded as imperfect, and the essence of man be such that it needed an improvement by means of a new revelation.

The essence of man is eternal and unchangeable. It could then seem more correct that the original revelation had become inactive as a consequence of man's misuse of his own freedom, and that God in love had given man his help. But at this it is asked how such a renewed revelation is possible, and how one can convince one's self that it is genuine.

The revelation is given either in an external way, through the senses, preferably sight. But if God thus has given man signs, these would only provide representations, and as soon as they would be developed into thought, they would be recognized as man's own; but the whole outer world is only a phenomenon of the spirit, and consequently not outside of him.

Or else this revelation could have occurred in an inner way—by inspiration, or effect on man's spirit, and not a development of what exists in man's own consciousness. This again involves the difficulty that one cannot understand how a thought can be placed in man's being, since every such [thought] is consciousness itself in a certain form or determination.

There are thus here three alternatives. Either man must have the capacity to apprehend what is deposited in him. This is, however, not exactly accepted by supranaturalism, since there would not be anything miraculous in it. Or man is said to receive with the revelation the mind and understanding to grasp it. But if he has not in his essence had the need of such, why then this change? Or finally, it is said that man's capacity is raised and developed in and at the revelation, so that this capacity becomes sufficient, though it did not exist before, or was insufficient.

This could be thought of as an external quickening, but by this revelation loses everything miraculous; and these external quickenings should be alike at all times, because one can see no reason why a certain time should have preference; and to think of the ability, once called forth, as again lost or destroyed, is absurd, because then the essence would be destroyed.

Revelation is, consequently, conceivable only if man has the ability to apprehend God; but then this is the thing itself, only undeveloped; God is everywhere present: why, then, should he not always be so in man? But, even if the original revelation is sufficient, this does not prevent the fact that there may be need of mighty revivals, which, appearing in time, receive the appearance of a higher divine revelation—but this is not extraordinary.

What next concerns the certainty about the nature of the divine revelation to comprise such a one, provided this certainty has been apprehended as in immediate experience, is that people have tried to explain and to retain it, either by something sensuous, and not divine, accompanying the revelation; or through something spiritual, an intuition, or a light shining in; or, by being transported, as it were, to a higher world.

This has, however, been attempted more by philosophers than by real theologians, who preponderantly have held themselves to the doctrine of inspiration.

Concerning these three methods it may be remarked that one can indeed convince one's self of a change within, but not about the fact that it comes from God, except by way of inference, as with the poets of ancient times; namely this that, because one is aware of things of which he is not aware at other times, and performs acts which are not done at other times, and that since they both are true and satisfying, therefore they come from God. This is correct to this extent that higher consciousness of what is true and right really are revelations from God.

But is this extraordinary? One may not be able to give the reason why it appeared just now; but this ground may possibly be the development of the race and of man's nature. But, on the other hand, it is difficult to know which revelation should be regarded as the true one, because all have their reasons. Therefore people have ascribed the reasons to immediate miracles. Those who have had revelations have discovered that they could perform deeds which at other times are not possible—which, therefore, have come from God.

With regard to such deeds we have already expressed

ourselves about miracles. Here the same is true as about creation, that of giving shape and form, but not of producing anything new. One wonders about that which one cannot understand; and thus there are miracles for man as a consequence of ignorance about the laws which exist for that which happens. The only miraculous thing is the whole, and the existence and power of the spirit itself.[25]

This is inexplicable, for otherwise the existing would be explained out of the non-existing. God's presence and activity in the sensuous world is only miraculous for the sensuous man. Further, if we should agree that someone performs miracles, it would not follow from it that he is supplied with, or does this in the power of, divine might; one must first discover him to be good and beautiful in his activity, because man's divinity consists in this. Consequently one must investigate and find that which has been said and done to be true by this, that one finds it to be rational. The miracles of the Bible here signify so much the less, because, for example, the magicians of Pharaoh performed miracles. This was a common thing at that time.

No revelation needs anything else to be recognized as divine than that it is true. The divine cannot be anything militating against the truth, neither can it be above reason, because this is a system above which nothing can exist. The whole controversy with regard to the point in question is based on the conception of the relationship between God and man.

Both parties—those who have affirmed, and those who have denied, miracles and special revelations—have believed that man was outside God, and thus worked with powers that are not his. Man would then be able to get

25. Perhaps it should be rendered "himself."

along without much knowledge that God needs, and what further knowledge might be attained by him would come from without. The strife is consequently easy to conciliate, when one knows the right relationship between God and man.

No supranaturalism has, furthermore, been consistent with this lower conception, because exegesis has always been admitted to be necessary. But this is impossible, if we do not believe that God is the true and that the true is God. It is only imagination when anyone believes himself to be a supranaturalist. When a person does not feel that he himself has the strength to search out the truth, then he accepts that which is presented from without. This is also correct in this sense that the revelation is divine, but it is not extraordinary, which latter one accepts when one thinks that God would permit man to pronounce the true without first reflecting upon it.

Outline of the Philosophy of Religion

OUTLINE OF THE PHILOSOPHY OF RELIGION[1]

Introduction

A. PROBLEMS

1.

WHAT is *The Philosophy of Religion?* In this question two others are included which must first be answered: (1) *What is philosophy?* (2) *What is religion?*

2.

Both of the latter questions may have a double meaning, or may be resolved into two others: (1) What are *philosophy and religion as such?* (2) What are they in relation to us, i.e. as man's philosophy and religion?[2] The relationship between these questions, the order of their being answered.[3]

3.

But even the second of these may be taken in a dual sense: (1) What have philosophy and religion *up to the present* been in relation to us? (2) What must they *always remain* in relation to us, as distinct from what they are considered absolutely? It is only in the second sense that the question is here considered.

1. The literal wording of the title is: "The Philosophy of Religious Doctrine." It is, however, equivalent to "Philosophy of Religion."
2. Sometimes Boström begins the sentence following a colon with a capital, and sometimes not. Consistent capitalization is followed in the translation.
3. Boström does not always use complete sentences in this *Outline*.

B. PHILOSOPHY CONSIDERED ABSOLUTELY

4.

From a *formal point of view* philosophy, considered absolutely, is: (a) a science, consequently α) a *knowledge,* a definite form of self-consciousness or *perceiving* together with a definite degree of *certainty* or conviction, β) a *systematic knowing,* a system of thoughts; (b) the *highest science* both α) *qualitatively* and β) *quantitatively,* when it is compared with the other sciences, for which it is the *foundation.*[4]

5.

From a *material point of view* philosophy, considered absolutely, is: (a) The science of the self-existing, of the *absolutely true being* or *essence,* consequently not of the phenomenon without regard to the former; (b) the science of the *concepts* or *ideas,* of the absolute reason and its substance,[5] which is exactly the absolutely true being.

6.

From this come the *most general (formal) attributes* in philosophy, when the word is taken in its absolute meaning. It is, namely, *a life* or *self-consciousness* with the attributes (a) *infinite,* consequently α) *absoluteness* and β) *organic pan-unity;*[6] (b) *immateriality,* consequently α) *spirituality* and β) *eternity.*

---

4. Literally: "For which it [philosophy] lies as *foundation.*"
5. The word used—"innehåll"—primarily means "content."
6. "All-enhet," for which "pan-unity" seems adequate.

C. HUMAN PHILOSOPHY[7]

7.

Philosophy for us, or human philosophy, is *possible* on condition of the postulate that man is: (1) *rational,* that is, a sharer in the absolute reason, a sharer in philosophy as such; (2) *finitely-rational,* that is, not completely but only more or less sharing in it. From this come the most *general attributes* in human philosophy in so far as it is considered in contrast with philosophy taken absolutely. Compare *6.*

8.

The philosophy which is *possible* for man therefore as a consequence always remains only relatively identical with the absolute philosophy; indeed it is possible only in so far as, and in the measure that, the absolute being, reason with its ideas, can appear and be grasped in the human self-consciousness and its world, in the relatively existing (the phenomenon), of which it is the substance and into which it enters as (a more or less potential or actual) *element.* Consequence of this for the character of human philosophy and for the *method,* by which the same can be achieved.

D. RELIGION IN THE ABSOLUTE AND RELATIVE SENSE

9.

Religion in itself, or in the absolute sense, can be nothing else than *the absolute being* or reason, which, nevertheless, *not merely as* such is called religion, except in so

7. Literally, "Man's Philosophy," though "Human Philosophy" may be a better rendering.

far as it is regarded as *binding* and in a certain way *determining or regulating* the spiritual being's *free activity;* in other words, as this activity's purpose and law. From this come the *most general attributes* of religion. Compare *6.*

10.

Again, as far as religion for us, or human religion, is concerned, it is possible under the same postulates and in the same degree as human philosophy, and its *most general attributes* are also analogous to those which belong to this one. *Human religion,* furthermore, is not only a knowing, but it is likewise and *essentially a willing and doing;* wherefore the philosophy of religion is at the same time a practical discipline.

E. INTRODUCTION TO PHILOSOPHY

11.

Human philosophy is (A) *theoretical* in so far as it conceives of the absolute being as the *final ground* for man and his world, and explains the latter through the former; (B) *practical* in so far as it conceives the same being as the *highest end* of man and his world, and determines his free activity in the way according to which this end can and should be attained.

12.

Theoretical philosophy has three divisions: (a) *theology,* (b) *anthropology,* and (c) *ethnology.* The object or substance of these is being, namely, man and the world in general for the first; the individual man for the second; and for the third, man naturally united, the tribe, the nation.

148

13.

Practical philosophy also has three divisions: (a) *philosophy of religion,* (b) *ethics,* and (c) *political science.* The object or content of the first is for the purpose of man in general, of the second for the individual man, and of the third for man collectively, the state. In addition to this it is taught in each division how the free human enterprise should be determined by the purpose that is indicated.[8]

14.

Remark: Anthropology and ethnology taken together may be called *cosmology* or *anthropology in a wide sense.* In like manner moral philosophy (ethics) and political science (statescraft) together may be called *jurisprudence in a wide sense.*

15.

The *philosophy of religion* must primarily determine the *concept* of religion or of the *religious life* with respect to form and content, as well as indicate the relative limitations which religion must meet in the finite man. This is the object of the true *philosophy of religion.*

16.

The same science must, furthermore, in general present the specific *forms of religion* in their relation to one another and to the concept of religion, as well as determine the *laws of their historical development,* which belongs to the *history of the philosophy of religion.*

---

8. The last two sentences are one in Boström. They are divided here in the interest of clarity.

17.

General remarks: Concerning the interest of the philosophy of religion in science and life; concerning its *relation* to the *positive science of religion;* concerning the relative necessity of permitting its presentation to be here preceded by that of theoretical philosophy, etc.

Theology

INTRODUCTORY REMARKS

18.

Is there a God?[9] And *what* is God? The relation of these questions to each other. What is God *taken absolutely?* And what is he *for us?* [The problem as] to what extent these question can be distinguished. Compare *8.*

19.

Remarks concerning the so called *proofs of the existence of God.* What has been intended by them. What should not have been intended by them. *The meaning of a proof.* The result of it for the question which is considered here, and the *progress of the present investigation.*

A. THE EXISTING

20.

What is *the existing in itself?* What must one imagine by this expression? The *existing* is the perceived; for *to be* is=*to be perceived.* Possible objections to this; their occasions and solution. The meaning of *an essence* or *a being in a wide sense* and of an *essence in a limited* or specific sense.

9. Literally, *"Is* God?"

21.

The *perceived,* the *existing* as such, cannot be anything else than self-consciousness and its attributes, i.e. *perceptions.* The substantial in everything is life or self-consciousness; everything is a definite modus or form of this, and beyond or independent of it there is absolutely nothing.

22.

Proofs of this proposition, taken (1) from *the simplicity of self-consciousness and its relationship* to everything that exists or is perceived; (2) from the very *idea of perception.* The reason why we human beings place *the perception* (the subjective) and *its objects* (the objective) against each other; (3) from the axiom that *nothing can exist* and be anything *for another* without existing *first (as an idea)* and existing as something *by itself.*

23.

Further evidence, taken (1) from the *relativity and the subjectivity of the sensuous reality.* Remark: Concerning the absurdities of *materialism* and *in specie* of *atomism;* (2) especially from the *significance of space* and its relation to us, i.e. to our spirit, and the impossibility that anything could exist beyond (extra) self-consciousness; (3) from *the impossibility to express in words* anything else than our own perceptions or to speak about anything else than these.

24.

Further evidence, taken (1) from *the impossibility to gain* any *knowledge* of the existing, in case it really were something else than perceptions, or were not such; (2) from *the course of human culture* in general and from the course of philosophical culture in particular; (3) from the fact that at least *the incompletely perceived* as such cannot be anything else than *perceptions,* and that these, nevertheless, are *more identical with self-existing* in the measure that they are less incomplete.

25.

Consequently, *the result of this,* namely, that the most general attribute, the first and the substantial in everything, is life and self-consciousness, that everything is a definite modus or form of this, and that without or independently of this nothing can be found. *Absolute idealism* is the only absolutely true view of the world.

B. THE NECESSITY OF THE ABSOLUTE REASON, OR THE EXISTENCE OF GOD

26.

Every form of life or self-consciousness is self-existing[10] or self-conscious in a definite way, i.e. perceives, or is a *rationality in a wide sense (mens, percipiens).* But this does not prevent it from *also being a perception (perceptio & perceptum),* namely, in another perceiving being, provided this one refers it to *itself* as *its* determination.[11] Further concerning the relationship between the perceiving being and its perceptions.

27.

Every form of self-consciousness, *every perceiving or rational being,* has *all the others* as its attributes, i.e. *as*

---

10. Boström's expression is "sjelf lefvande"—"self-living," but "self-existing" seems better form and adequately represents the original.

11. "Bestämning." Other English equivalents of this word are "attribute," "quality," and "property."

its perceptions, so that in reality all is in all, ἐν παντί πάντα. Remarks concerning the *monadology* of Leibniz, and what is satisfactory in it or the contrary.

28.

Taken together, *the rational* beings also comprise an organic whole or *a system* in which each one has a definite degree of perfection in relation to the whole and stands in definite relationships to each one of the others; from which it follows that there is *only one single world,* when it is viewed *in its truth and perfection.*

29.

But *not every* being grasps *all* the others *with the same completeness* or just as really. In this respect there can and must be an infinity of gradations. For this reason each one, in addition, *has actu its own and altogether distinct world,* irrespective of the extent to which it may be identical with that of the others and with the only absolutely true, of which it is a relatively perfect conception.[12]

30.

Since, therefore, relative and *imperfect conceptions exist,* and since these are *not* possible *without the assumption of perfect ones,* which again are impossible without some one who perceives perfectly, the reality and *necessity of an absolutely perceiving being* is thereby presented, i.e. presented *by reason* κατ' ἐξοχὴν which, in conformity with its idea, cannot be more than *just one; this is God.*

---

12. This entire paragraph is one sentence in the original, divided in only one place by a semicolon. For easier English, it is here broken up into several sentences.

31.

Observations concerning the chief of the so called *proofs of the existence of God,* concerning the *ontological,* the *cosmological,* the *teleological,* and the *ethico–theological.* The critiques by Kant and others of these proofs. In what measure they are valid or not, and why.

C. GENERAL LOGICAL DETERMINATIONS OR ATTRIBUTES OF THE ABSOLUTE REASON

32.

The importance of the words *attributes* or *qualities.* The *importance* and the *difficulty* of the doctrine concerning God's attributes. How and why a plurality of them may be regarded as possible.[13]

33.

The *division of the divine attributes* into: (A) *logical,* which are (a) *formal,* (b) *real,* which again are in part α) *ontological,* in part β) *noological;* (B) *metaphysical,* which are (a) *aetiological,* (b) *teleological.* Observations concerning the relationship to each other of these kinds of attributes.

34.

The *first class* of the logical attributes comprise the formal, or the *attributes of infiniteness* of the divinity, which are (a) *absoluteness,* i.e. α) *independence,*[14] abso-

13. Boström's own word for "them" is "such."
14. The word used here is identical with the German "Unabhängigkeit." The two words used by Boström mean about the same thing, although the second may be a bit stronger and thus the rendering, "absolute self-existence."

lute self-existence, β) *perfection,* positive infiniteness; (b) *organic pan-unity,*[15] i.e. α) *unity in the many,* β) *the many*[16] *in unity,* consequently infinite harmony.

35.

The *second class* of the logical attributes consists of the *ontological,* or the *attributes concerning the reality* of God, which are (a) absolute *immateriality,* or the quality of transcending sense,[17] i.e. α) *spirituality,* β) *eternity;* (b) *substantiality, having the quality of an organism,*[18] i.e. α) *quality of universal being,*[19] omnipresence, β) *om-nipotence.*

36.

The *third class* of logical attributes consists of the *noological,* or God's *attributes of ideality,* which are (a) *absolute knowing,* i.e. α) *self-consciousness,* β) *omnis-cience;* (b) *absolute rationality,* i.e. α) *personality* and β) *complete personality.*[20]

37.

These three classes are embraced respectively by the attributes: (A) *beauty* in the wide sense—majesty, (a) *sublimity,* (b) *beauty* in a narrow sense; (B) *truth,* (a) *sub-stance,* (b) the *quality of universal being,*[21] systematic

15. Again the word "all-enhet"—"all-oneness." In Swedish, combinations are very common, and it is often difficult to give them in idiomatic English.

16. "Allhet"—literally, "all-ness." This is another coined word. The context indicates that Boström has "many" in mind.

17. I.e. "supersensuality," or the supersensuous.

18. "Organiskhet"—literally, "organicism-hood."

19. "Allväsenhet"—literally, "all-beinghood."

20. The combination "allpersonlighet" would mean a personality that fills the universe—"all-inclusive personality."

21. See note 19.

quality of universal being; (C) *goodness,* (a) *life,* (b) *blessedness.* All of them must here be regarded in the absolute sense.[22]

38.

Further *observations* concerning the *negative* and *positive* expressions of these attributes; concerning their consequences; concerning the critical evaluation of them by Strauss and others, and to what extent this may be regarded valid, etc.

D. THE COMPREHENSION OR IDEAS OF THE ABSOLUTE BEING

39.

The *inner determination* or *comprehension* of the absolute reason consists of its perceptions, its *ideas* or *conceptions,* which here are regarded only as thought in and by their absolute subject.

40.

Every idea, thus thought, is the absolute reason itself, regarded in a certain determination, in a certain form of its infinite life or self-consciousness. This self, however, must *not* be regarded as being only the *combination* of its ideas, so that it would be completely identical with its contents.

41.

Every idea, as such, has the same general determination, the same attributes, as the absolute reason; but it also has another and *special determination,* through which it is distinguished from it, as well as from every other idea.

22. A phrase is here made into a complete sentence.

42.

Every *idea requires all* the others together with their subject in order to be what it is. It is the whole considered from a certain point of view, and it is *a certain unity for us of all the others,* which comprise its content and refer themselves to it either as its *positive* or *negative determinations.*

43.

By itself, i.e. as thought in and by God, *every idea is absolutely perfect (40);* but this does not prevent the possibility of comparing the ideas with each other *with regard to their special determination* alone, and that then the one is more complete than the other in the sense that the one has more positive and fewer negative determinations than the other.

44.

Therefore also God,[23] when compared with the other beings, has *only positive attributes,* and not a single negative one. If we properly ascribe to him *negative attributes,* these would only be negations of negatives and consequently actually positive. The meaning of the scholastic expressions, *ens perfectissimum, realissimum,* the *highest being,* etc.

45.

An idea can be thought not only as existing within oneself, as far as its own positive content is concerned, but also as existing *in others,* who are *higher* or *more perfect,* and into whom it must enter as a positive determination. Regarded in this latter way, *it itself also* re-

23. Boström's word is "divinity," but the context clearly indicates that he means God.

ceives a *greater* determination, and this applies in the same measure even more, the higher the idea is within which it is thought.

46.

From this it follows that *all ideas* have their *complete determination* and significance in the measure in which they are thought of in and by the absolute reason.[24] It also follows that their *original tendency* as well as their *highest end and good* must be to live and compose oneself in and through this, provided they themselves are living and perceiving beings. *All other tendencies* and *ends* properly stand in relation to this end as inferior moments and means.

47.

Beyond that man has *no special knowledge about God's ideas as such,* but only to the extent that they comprise positive determinations in man himself, in which case they nevertheless reveal themselves as his, that is, they belong to the relative world. *About God's idea of himself* he [man] has only a relative consciousness; and any higher idea than this cannot fall within *his* world.

E. THE RELATIVE SUBSTANTIALITY

48.

If *the ideas are attributed to God,* i.e. are thought of by him, they are *his* ideas or perceptions, and it is only he who then is self-conscious with regard to them, only he that comprises their eternal essence and substance. They also concern him alone, without any other beings than he being determined by them.

24. "I och af."

158

49.

But *if they also* can and must *be attributed to themselves,* and are subjected to self-scrutiny, *each one of* them is, however, *also for himself living* and self-conscious in a determinate way, in other words, a perceiving or *rational being,* a *personality;* for under no other condition either would or could they be perceptions of the absolute reason.

50.

If one should ask *what they,* as perceiving beings, *apprehend or perceive,* it would be true with regard to them also that they cannot perceive anything else than *themselves and their perceptions* in their individual determination; and since in their essence they are organic moments in the system of divine ideas, consequently each one of them is this system itself, regarded from a certain special point of view, and therefore they also have this as the *original* and *eternal* content of their self-consciousness, provided they are considered in their truth and perfection.

51.

But since they not only are perceiving, but also finite, beings, therefore they cannot grasp their essential substance with the same completeness as the infinite reason, indeed, the one among them cannot grasp it with the same perfection as the other; consequently the same substance, *the world of the beings or ideas,* must reveal itself to each of them as something different or the opposite of what it is for itself (for God) and for all the others, i.e. they must find and possess *another reality* as *theirs* than the one which exists immediately for God.

52.

Consequently, then, there exists *for them,* in addition to the absolute reality or world, a *relative reality,* which *also* consists of as *many relatively distinct worlds* as there are finitely perceiving beings, because *these worlds are nothing* but the finite beings as they are self-conscious in their complete relative determination, consequently always altogether dissimilar and individual, no matter to what extent they may be partially identical.

53.

The *relative reality,* or, since only that of man is known to us, *our relative world* is thus a *phenomenon,* an incomplete perception *of the absolute,* which, as essence, is its foundation, and also in that respect *is* or *is perceived,* although not completely as it is in its verity, but *more or less* differently, according to the manner in which it is grasped, whether less or more completely.

54.

The *relative world* may indeed *as a whole* have *determinations* or attributes which are the very *opposite* of those which belong to the absolute *(34–37);* but since *this antithesis is merely relative,* it does not prevent the former from being *partially more or less identical* with the latter. Further development of this relationship, and thereby *explanation* of the most general attributes *of the phenomenon.*

55.

The *relative world* is *everywhere* a *unity of contradictions,* namely, of the being, through all its attributes *(34–37)* and *of its negation* in the same manner as the former reveals itself in the phenomenon as its *potential infinity,* even though this is in all of its moments *as actually finite.* From this comes the *unlimited development of the phenomenon,* which constitutes one of its essential characteristics.

56.

Since *the unity of contradictions* within the phenomenal world *permeates the whole,* therefore all of its parts must stand in what has been called *a state of polarity* to each other, so that when two distinct phenomena are compared with each other, the essence will appear relatively more and the opposite or negation of the essence will appear less in the one than in the other. A reminder in this connection of *Schelling's way* of *determining the absolute* in his system of identity.

57.

Comparison of the view of the universe presented here with others, in particular those of more recent date. *Evidence* that the former *cannot properly* be called *pantheistic,* or lead to the consequences which must be regarded as valid reasons for discarding pantheism.

The Metaphysical Attributes of God

58.

The *relative world* does *not lie within* the absolute world in the sense that it comprises a constituent part of it; but neither does it lie *outside of it* in the sense that it is independent of it. A *relationship* thus exists between them, when they are considered from the point of view of the former [view]; and a consideration of God under this circumstance belongs to *metaphysics,* the general foundation of which is given in what precedes *(48–56).*

59.

According to what already has been evidenced, *the relative world is a secondary existence,*[25] which for its possible existence[26] and reality *postulates another* as its *ground;* and since besides the relative existence there is no other than the absolute, i.e. God, therefore he must comprise the ground of the relative world in all the considerations and from all the viewpoints from which it can be regarded.

60.

But as finitely-infinite *(55)* the relative world is *one continually evolving reality,* and therefore it can be considered with respect to (A) *its reality* and from this point of view in regard to (a) its material and formal *existence* as such and (b) its *existence* or *continuation* in its existence; (B) its *development* and from this point of view with respect to (a) its *form* of development and (b) the *goal of* its development and direction.

61.

If, therefore, God is considered in relation to the *reality* of the *relative world,* and, furthermore, only from the *ontological* point of view *(35),* he is this world's *primordial being*[27] and as such (a) its *cause*[28] (original cause) and (b) its *original substance,*[29] even though, as absolute, he is this only indirectly and mediately. It is to be observed that here we are not concerned with any

25. The word here rendered "secondary" could also mean "subordinate."

26. Literally, "possibility."

27. "Urväsende," the same as the German "Urwesen."

28. "Orsak." In parenthesis Boström has "ursak," which would be the same as the German "Ursache."

29. "Ursubstans."

empirical causality or substantiality, but only with a rational.

62.

And when he is further considered in the same relationship, but, in addition, from a *noological* point of view, a consideration that includes and enlarges upon the previous one, then he is the *original intelligence*[30] of the relative world, and as such (a) its *creator* and (b) *sustainer* in which case the same remark holds true as above *(61)*. The impossibility of a *creation in time*. The possible meaning of a *creation out of nothing*. The question of the *purpose* of creation, etc.

63.

If again God is considered in relation to the *development* of the relative world, and, further, only from an *ontological point of view,* he is, nevertheless, by implication and mediately, the *source of religion*[31] of the same world and as such its (a) highest *law* and (b) highest *end,* which thus is realized infinitely, even though in each of its moments only in a finite way.

64.

And if he is regarded in the same relationship from the *noological point of view,* he is in the same manner the *absolute regent* of the relative world, and as such (a) its *highest providence* and (b) its most complete savior,[32] in which regard our world can be considered as one of his realms, in connection with which the preceding remark *(63)* should not be overlooked.

30. "Ur-intelligens."
31. "Ur-religion."
32. The literal expression is "highest savior," but "most complete savior" seems a more adequate translation.

65.

Thought of in the latter relationship *(63, 64)* God has the attributes of *holiness* and *righteousness,* and further of *omniscience* and *goodness*[33] for us. These attributes possess only *metaphysical* significance and express his logical being in special relationship to man, who as self-conscious, free, and rational, stands in a more immediately intimate relationship to him than everything else that exists in his world.[34]

Anthropology

A. CONCERNING MAN IN GENERAL

66.

Man, inwardly regarded,[35] is a relatively rational, *a sensuously rational being,* and as such distinguished not only from God himself, but also from that idea in him which is the most immediate ground of man's being. Further analysis of what is implied by this.

67.

This formal explanation concerns *not only* the individual human being, but also *humanity* in all its states. *The human organism,* furthermore, should not be regarded as alone constituting the *sensuous* human being. *The entire sensuous world,* as seen from man's point of view, should be regarded as belonging to his phenomenal existence and comprising his determinateness.

---

33. The word Boström uses here is "allgodhet." Swedish has great facility for such combinations, which usually are difficult, and sometimes impossible, to convey into English in the richness of the original.

34. This paragraph is one sentence in the original.

35. Literally, "considered within himself."

68.

The *attributes* which belong to man as a consequence of his general concept[36] *(66)* are *already stated* in what precedes and are to be found by combining *55* with *34–37*. The *relationship* in man, furthermore, between *the being and the phenomenon,* between reason and sensuousness, is determined according to the analogy of God's relationship to the relative in general, concerning which see *61–64.* Further particulars about this relationship when the being is considered *within* the phenomenon and vice versa.

69.

It is *especially* observed that man is temporal, or, more correctly, *eternally-temporal,*[37] consequently becoming, inconstant, *a life in continuous development,* a determination which must be explained through the relative finiteness of his ideas in connection with the organic nature of his determinations (those of the other ideas).

70.

As a consequence of this determination man is to be regarded as a *living activity* or an *active life;* and, furthermore, since man everywhere is a *unity of contradictions (55, 56),* therefore also his activity must reveal itself as such, i.e. in part as *more active* and in part as *more passive,* as the being expresses itself more or less.

71.

But *all activity has a purpose* for which it struggles, and this can be nothing else than *the concept of the active being (66);* consequently man as active cannot tend to

36. Here the meaning appears to be the concept of man.
37. The hyphenated expression is "evigt-timlig."

anything else than that he, *though sensuous, may become rational;* that he may live and comprehend himself as a unity of the rational and the sensuous through the change of the latter, which would imply his own change; for the rational is inherently unchangeable.

72.

What, furthermore, man thus strives for he can *attain actually to a greater or less degree,* in part involuntarily, as a consequence of his original ability[38] and his finiteness, and in part voluntarily, as a consequence of his morality or his immorality. But this does not prevent the *tendency, considered as a matter of principle,* from being always *the same;* it is only its *direction and use,* only its closer determination in every moment of life, that determines to what degree and in what manner the total is reached.

73.

Even the *general trend* of man's development depends on the fact that *its content* is in part relatively more general, and in part relatively more particular, and that *the former* must be regarded by him as relatively *more central, inner, present,* and *the latter* as relatively *more peripheral, exterior, absent,* not only to the extent that it coexists in space, but also to the extent that it follows in time.

74.

This, added to the fact of man's finiteness, explains why man, considered in a definite period of his life, is *originally more external* and unconscious, and that he from this point *in due time changes so that he becomes*

38. Boström's word here is "Mått"—"measure." The context makes it clear, however, that he means "measure of ability."

more introspective[39] and self-conscious until he reaches his *culmination,* as well as the fact that thereafter he *gradually reverts* to a more external and unconscious condition, etc.; all of this takes place provided that the development is normal and is not interrupted by contingent circumstances.

75.

Finally, it is observed that man's general work in time is a continued *reflecting* with which, as a consequence of his finiteness, there is united a likewise continued *abstracting* in the negative significance of this word. The word has another meaning when it designates the opposite to the *determination,* in which case it expresses the progress of reflection from the more concrete to the more abstract.

B. CONCERNING MAN'S FUNCTIONS AND CAPACITIES

76.

What man is when he is considered in a certain undivided moment of his activity or of his active life is called *one of his functions* or *manifestations,* which is consequently not to be regarded merely as *one activity,* but also as *one effect, one product,* of his being. Remarks concerning the ground and fitness of the determination.

77.

Such a function or manifestation is also always to be regarded as *a unity in multiplicity,* both with regard to its content and the period of time it occupies; it can, therefore, be regarded, according to preference, both as

39. The word "inre"—"inner"—is translated as "instrospective," which better conveys the full meaning.

one single function and as a plurality of such, concerning each one of which the same would then apply, etc.

78.

Both the possibility and the reality of all the functions of man depend primarily on his eternal being, which, regarded in this relation to them, i.e. as their ground and unity and subject, is called *capacity* or *ability* in general, but in the same relationship to a *certain kind* among them, *a* (certain) *capacity* or *an ability* of *this* kind of functions, which relate themselves to him in general as the higher to the lower. Compare *68*.

79.

From this it is thus apparent that *all power or ability* is *that of the being* or of the spirit; but *in specie* such a power is, nevertheless, called a faculty of the mind, provided that man expresses himself in it as *soul*, i.e. as *actu* or perceptibly self-conscious and independent. Remarks: Concerning the *difficulties* which we have been wont to find in the assumption of individual faculties of the mind, and how they can be settled; further, concerning the ground of the classification of the human capacities and their significance, etc.

80.

With regard to (I) the *form* of his functions and his activity man is (A) an *elemental being,* i.e. *imperceptibly* self-conscious or perceiving and as such either abstract or qualified or organized matter; (B) *spiritual being,* i.e. perceptibly self-conscious or perceiving; and it is to be observed in this connection that *the lower* form is *always in connection* with the higher, when it is developed. The difference, however, is relative, depending on a more or a less. Consideration of the consequences of this.

168

81.

As a spiritual being, man is (a) *perceiving* and *spontaneous,* noticeable to others, but not to himself; (b) *conscious* and *arbitrary,* noticeable to himself, but not as spirit; (c) *self-conscious* and *free,* noticeable also to himself as spirit. The same comment as above is valid here. The content itself is richer or more concrete in the same degree (potentially) as the form is lower or less spiritual, which is a consequence of man's finitude.

82.

With regard to (II) *the content* of his functions and his activity man is (a) *sensuous* or, considered as ability, *sensuousness;* (b) *rational,* or, considered as ability, *reason.* The opposition between the two capabilities is the same as between the being and the phenomenon. *Neither* can exist in the actual man *without* or *exterior to* the *other.* At the beginning, however, the former appears as predominating.[40]

83.

With regard to (III) the *purpose* or *direction* of his functions man is (a) *theoretical ability,* provided that he predominantly intends *higher self-consciousness* through development[41] of the soul; (b) *practical ability,* provided that he predominantly intends *higher freedom* through development of the exterior; (c) *esthetic ability,* provided that he predominantly intends *merely pleasure or diversion* through activity as such.

40. One sentence in the original is here divided into two.
41. The word used means "change," but the context indicates the kind of change that implies development.

84.

Remarks concerning the *relation* of these *divisions* to each other, especially concerning the *theoretical, practical,* and *esthetic* capacities, their *appelations in Swedish,* their relationship to each other and to the *general purpose,* their bases and results, as well as what is gained by it, etc.

C. CONCERNING MAN'S THEORETICAL ABILITY

85.

The sensuous theoretical ability is (a) *sensuous power to feel,* or *sense in a lower signification* (as that of the animal), which expresses itself as α) *vital-sense*[42] for measures[43] of pleasure or displeasure; β) *the sense of the organs,* the higher, with its familiar modifications: the *five exterior senses.* The very expressions of this ability are called *feelings in a wider sense* and objective feelings or *organ-sensations,* which together comprise the qualities of the reality existing in *space.*

86.

The same ability, furthermore, develops into (b) *ability to foreshadow,* which is α) *sense in a higher degree* (as human) provided it has the same content as the ability to feel, but considers it as an object opposite to itself; β) *power of imagination,* provided it has another content than merely the ability to feel, an inner, clearer, more idealistic and more arbitrary world, which partially corresponds to the external, more vital and necessary objec-

42. "Vital-sinne." Boström's use of "vital" is apparently Latin, and is left thus.
43. Boström uses only the word "modi." It is seemingly the plural of the Latin "modus."

tive [world], and *is not only* in the *presently represented space,* but *also in time.* The functions of sense are called *awarenesses,*[44] *intuitions;* [the functions] of the power of imagination in the essential sense [are called] *representations.*

87.

As power of imagination the spirit can more or less arbitrarily use its represented content and (1) *reproduce* it in accordance with *associations,* (2) *transform* it according to the law of *fashion*[45] and *schematize* it according to the laws of *generalization,* after which the power of imagination also receives *distinct appellations.* *Remarks:* Concerning the meaning, conditions, and limitations of these activities. Further, concerning *memory,* and concerning the meaning of *space* and *time* and the *organic* body.

88.

The sensuous theoretical power further develops into (c) the *power of thought* or *reason in a wide sense,* which is α) *concrete power of thought,* provided at the same time that its content is that of the power of presentation, though clearer, evident, inner, spiritual, fundamental, necessary, and immutable, though at the same time not completed; β) *abstract* or *pure power of thought,* provided its content is purely spiritual, and only needs *the language* to be realized. The functions of the former are properly called *abstract apprehensions,* relatively distinguished from schemata; those of the latter, *essential concepts.*

---

44. Though perhaps somewhat odd, this word is expressive of what Boström says here.

45. "Fictionens," which is apparently from "fingo," "to form," "to fashion."

GLOSSARY

natur—*nature*
objektiv—*objective*
omfatta—*apprehend, comprehend, embrace*
omätlig—*infinite*
ontologi—*ontology*
oändlig—*infinite*
panteism—*pantheism*
potentialitet—*potentiality*
praktisk—*practical*
realitet—*reality*
religion—*religion*
rätt, rättsvetenskap—*law*
sanning—*truth*
sedlig—*moral*
sinne—*mind*
sinnebild—*symbol*
sinnlighet—*sensuousness*
själ—*spirit*
självmedvetande—*consciousness*
skepnad—*form*
subjektiv—*subjective*
substans—*substance*

syfte—*purpose*
symbol—*symbol*
sätt—*nature*
tankeförmåga—*mind*
teism—*theism*
teologi—*theology*
teoretisk—*theoretical*
tillbedjan—*worship*
tillvaro—*being*
tro, troslära, trosbekännelse—*faith, creed*
uppenbarelse—*revelation*
uppoffring, uppoffra—*sacrifice*
varelse—*essence, being*
verklighet—*actuality, reality, substance, truth*
verksamhet—*activity*
vetande—*knowledge*
vetenskap—*science*
vilja—*will*
väsen—*substance, nature, being*
ändamål—*purpose*
ändlös—*infinite*

SELECTED BIBLIOGRAPHY

In the text, books and articles are referred to by the author's last name and the standard abbreviation of his work. Italic Arabic numerals refer to volumes, regular Arabic numerals to pages. The abbreviation "tr." means either "translator" or "translated by"; "ed." means either "edition," "editor," or "edited by." Other abbreviations are self-explanatory. This bibliography provides a selected and annotated survey of the literature by and about Boström and serves as a key to the abbreviations used in this book.

Aall, Anathon.—*FN*
Filosofien i norden. Kristiania: I Kommission hos Jacob Dybwad, 1919.
A presentation of philosophy as it has developed in the Scandinavian countries.
Beck, Lars Herman.—*RLB*
A Comparison of the Doctrines of Reality in the Philosophies of Lotze and Boström. Unpublished Doctor's dissertation, Yale University, New Haven, 1892.
Valuable for its clarity of presentation.
Borelius, Johan Jacob.—*KBF*
Kritik öfver den Boströmska filosofien. Stockholm: P. & Z. Heggströms förlag, 1859–1860.
Critical examination of Boström's thought.
Boström, Christopher Jacob.—*FE*
Föreläsningar i etiken (efter det muntlisa föredraget upptecknade och redigerade af Sigurd Ribbing). Upsala: Almqvist & Wiksells boktryckeri-aktiebolag, 1897.
Boström lectures in ethics as recorded and edited by Sigurd Ribbing.
————*FR*
Föreläsningar i religionsfilosofi (upptecknade och utgifna af Sigurd Ribbing). Stockholm: P. A. Nordstedt & söners förlag, 1885.
The book from which the translation in this book is made.
————*SB*
Skrifter af Christopher Jacob Boström. 3 vols. (vols. *1* and *2* ed. H. Edfeldt; *3* ed. H. Edfeldt and G. J. Keijser). *1* and *2*, Upsala: Victor Roos, 1883. *3*, Stockholm: Adolf Johnsons förlag, 1901.
Contains Boström's collected works together with introductory articles by H. Edfeldt.

Dons, Waldemar.—*OB*

Om Bostrømianismen. Christiania: A. W. Brøgger, 1874.
A critical study of Boström's philosophy from a Hegelian view-point.

Edfeldt, Hans.—*Festskrift*
"Christopher Jacob Boströms bevis för den absoluta idealismens nödvändighet och sanning." In [Keijser, ed.], *Festskrift*, 223–61.
A good discussion of absolute idealism.

————*DBF*
Granskning af kandidaten Waldemar Dons framställning af den Boströmska filosofien af E-f-t. Upsala: Esaias Edquists boktryck-eri, 1875.
A defense of Boström's position and reply to the critique by Waldemar Dons.

————*OBI*
Om Boströms idéelära. Upsala: Victor Roos, 1884.
A study of Boström's doctrine of ideas in controversy with A. Nyblaeus.

Hegel, G. W. F.—*LPR*
Lectures on the Philosophy of Religion (tr. E. B. Speirs and J. Burdon Sanderson) (ed. E. B. Speirs). 2nd ed. 3 vols. London: Kegan Paul, Trench, Trübner & Co., Ltd., 1895.

————*PM*
Philosophy of Mind (tr. William Wallace). Oxford: At the Clarendon Press, 1894.

Höffding, Harald.—*FS*
Filosofien i Sverige. Stockholm: P. A. Norstedt & söners, 1879.
A critical evaluation of Swedish philosophy with special at-tention to Boström.

Kalling, Pehr.—*FABF*
Framställning af Boströmska filosofien. Örebro: Abr. Bohlin, 1868.
Brief presentation of Boström's philosophical system.

————*OK*
Om kunskapen. Upsala: Essaias Edquist, 1875.
A study of epistemology from the idealistic point of view.

[Keijser, G. J., ed.]—*Festskrift*
Festskrift. Stockholm: P. A. Norstedt & söners förlag, 1897.
To the memory of C. J. Boström, 1797–1897. Contains: fac-simile of part of a letter from Boström to Nyblaeus, 1865;

thirty-one chapters by different writers; and a bibliography covering the years 1824–1897. Also contains festive song by C. D. of Wirsén. Name of editor is not given, but Vannérus says that it was G. J. Keijser (*BTF*, 192).

Landström, Gustaf D. R.—*OTB*
Om tänkaren Kristoffer Jacob Boström och hans filosofi. Stockholm: P. A. Norstedt & söners förlag, 1903.
> A lengthy, popular, clear, and appreciative lecture on the life and thought of Boström. Also contains some criticism.

Larsson, Hans.—*MÖB*
Minnesteckning över Christopher Jacob Boström. Stockholm: Albert Bonniers förlag, 1931.
> Largely biographical. Contains many interesting personal items and a brief presentation of Boström's philosophical system. A popularly written book that weaves intimate things of his life into the general structure of his thoughts.

Leander, Pehr Jolian Herman.—*LGI*
Boströms lära om Guds idéer; studier. Lund: Malmstrom & Kompis boktryckeri, 1886.
> Critical study dealing with the nature and significance of Boström's thought.

Liljeqvist, Efraim.—*BÄLD*
Boströms äldsta latinska dissertationer försvenskade af Efraim Liljeqvist. Lund: Håkan Ohlssons boktryckeri, 1915.
> Translation of Boström's oldest Latin dissertations.

——*BÄS*
Om Boströms ädsta skrifter. Göteborg: Wald, Zachrissons boktryckeri, 1897.
> Investigation of the genius of Boström's idealism. A careful work with excellent documentation.

Linder, Nils.—*Festskrift*
"Boströms behandling af modersmålet." In [Keijser, ed.], *Festskrift*, 379–82.
> A brief evaluation of Boström's style and diction.

Ljunghoff, Johannes.—*BSP*
Christopher Jacob Boström Sveriges Platon. Upsala: Almqvist & Wiksells boktryckeri, 1916.
> A popular and appreciative representation from a religious point of view. Well documented. Published under the auspices of Sweden's Christian Student Movement.

Lundeberg, Axel.—Art. (1927)
"Sweden's Contribution to Philosophy." *The Open Court, 41* (1927), 410–23.
> Summary and evaluation of Boström's philosophy included in a survey of Swedish thought.

Nosco, John.—*GPB*
"God in the Philosophy of Christopher Jacob Boström." Unpublished dissertation, Columbia University, 1957.
> A study of central tenets in Boström's thought.

Nyblaeus, Axel.—*Festskrift*
"Bidrag till en karakteristik af den Boströmska filosofien." In [Keijser, ed.], *Festskrift*, 1–16.
> A splendid, brief summary of Boström's idealism.

———*FFS*
Den filosofiska forskningen i Sverige. 4 vols. Lund: C. W. K. Gleerups förlag, vol. *1,* 1879; *2,* 1881; *3,* 1886; *4,* part 1, 1895; part 2, 1897.
> A history of philosophical research in Sweden.

———*TUBF*
Tvänne uppsatser om den Boströmska filosofien. Lund: C. W. K. Gleerups förlag, 1885.
> A study of the place of the ideas in Boström's philosophy.

[Pira, Karl and G. J. Keijser, eds.]—*SS*
Smärre Skrifter. 10 vols. Stockholm: Boströmsförbundet, 1908–17.
> Publications by the Boström society, perpetuating the thought and memory of Boström.

Ribbing, Sigurd (ed.).—*FE*
Professor Chr. Jac. Boströms föreläsningar i etiken. Upsala: Almquist & Wiksells boktryckeri-aktiebolag, 1897.
> See under Boström.

———*FR*
Chr. Jac. Boströms föreläsningar i religionsfilosofi. Stockholm: P. A. Norstedt & söners förlag, 1885.
> See under Boström.

Sahlin, Carl Yngve.—*Festskrift*
"Om filosofiens metod enligt Boströms åsikt." In [Keijser, ed.], *Festskrift*, 360–78.
> A study of philosophical method from Boström's position.

———*KSB*
Kants, Schleiermachers och Boströms etiska grundtankar. Upsala: Akademiska boktryckeriet, Ed. Berling, 1877.
> A study of the ethics of Kant, Schleiermacher, and Boström.

BIBLIOGRAPHY

Vannérus, Allen.—*BTF*
Till Boströms teoretiska filosofi en kritisk studie. Stockholm:
Albert Bonniers förlag, 1897.
  A critical study and appreciation of Boström. Popular in
  style. A beginner's introduction to Boström's philosophy.
Wedberg, Anders.—*LSBF*
Den logiska strukturen hos Boströms filosofi. Upsala: Almqvist
& Wiksell boktryckeri-A.-B., 1937.
  A recent careful and critical study of the logical structure of
  Boström's philosophy.
Wikner, Pontus.—*STB*
Om den svenske tänkaran Boström. Göteborg: Handelstidning
Aktiebolags tryckeri, 1888.
  A sympathetic presentation of Boström and his philosophy by
  one of his most outstanding students.
Zöller, Egon.—*Festskrift*
"Werden Wir Einmal für Uns das Sein, was Wir für Gott Sind?"
In [Keijser, ed.], *Festskrift,* 112–17.
  A study of man's development toward his idea in God.
[1]Åberg, L. H.—*BV*
*Den Boströmska verldsåsigten i sina grunddrag framställd af L.
H. Åberg.* Stockholm: Ivar Heggströms boktryckeri, 1882.
  A study of the fundamental elements in Boström's world view.
Åkesson, Elof.—*FIL*
Filosofien. Eftertryck ur Sverige i våra dagar BDI. (Stockholm:
Aktiebolaget, 1927.) Lund: Skånska centraltryckeriet, 1934.
  A brief study of philosophy in Sweden.

1. In the Swedish alphabet the concluding letters are å, ä, and ö.

INDEX